THE
DOUBLEDAY BOOK
OF
FAMOUS
AMERICANS

SUZANNE LEVERT

DOUBLEDAY

NEW YORK   LONDON   TORONTO   SYDNEY   AUCKLAND

To my favorite nephew and nieces (in order of appearance):
Michael, Catherine, Annie, and Lydia, with much love.
S.L.

Photo Credits: pages 1, 4, 10, 13, 16, 28, 43, 52, 58, 64, 67, 79, 85, 103, 109, 112, 115, 124,
130, 133, 142, 151, 154, 160, 166, 169, 176, 189, 195, 198, 201, 204, 223, 238, 241, 263,
266, 269, 272, 284, 299, 302, and 305, courtesy of AP/Wide World Photos, reprinted with
permission; page 97, courtesy of H. Roger Viollet, reprinted with permission; pages 37, 94, and
157, courtesy of the New York Public Library Picture Collection; all other photos courtesy of the
Library of Congress.

COVER CREDITS

1	President Harry Truman	Globe Photos
2	Amelia Earhart	Culver Pictures
3	Bob Dylan	AP/Wide World
4	George Gershwin	Culver Pictures
5	Walter Cronkite	AP/Wide World
6	Louis Armstrong	AP/Wide World
7	Clara Barton	Library of Congress
8	Walt Whitman	Library of Congress
9	Charles Lindbergh	Culver Pictures
10	Martha Graham	UPI/Bettmann Newsphotos
11	Abraham Lincoln	Library of Congress
12	Joe Namath	AP/Wide World
13	Martin Luther King Jr.	Globe Photos
14	Sitting Bull	Library of Congress
15	Frederick Douglass	Library of Congress
16	Thomas Alva Edison	Culver Pictures
17	Gloria Steinem	AP/Wide World
18	Katharine Hepburn	Culver Pictures
19	Eugene O'Neill	Library of Congress
20	Jackie Robinson	AP/Wide World
21	Sandra Day O'Connor	Library of Congress
22	Bruce Springsteen	AP/Wide World
23	John McEnroe	AP/Wide World
24	Bill Cosby	AP/Wide World

1	2	3	4	5
6				7
8				9
10	11	12	13	14
15	16	17	18	19
20	21	22	23	24

Published by Doubleday, a division of Bantam Doubleday Dell Publishing Group, Inc. 666 Fifth
Avenue, New York, New York 10103.   **Doubleday** and the portrayal of an anchor with a
dolphin are trademarks of Doubleday, a division of Bantam Doubleday Dell Publishing Group,
Inc.   Library of Congress Cataloging-in-Publication Data   LeVert, Suzanne, 1958– The
Doubleday book of famous Americans / by Suzanne LeVert.— 1st ed. p.   cm. Includes index.
Summary: Profiles 101 famous Americans from all walks of life (history, politics, sports, science,
movies, etc.) and from the 1600s to the present.   ISBN 0-385-23699-9   1. United States—
Biography—Juvenile literature. 2. United States—Biography—Portraits—Juvenile literature. [1.
United States—Biography.]   I. Title. CT217.L39   1989 920′.073—dc19 [B] [920]
87-26215   CIP   AC

DESIGNED BY / DIANE STEVENSON / SNAP•HAUS GRAPHICS

C O N T E N T S

CONTENTS

CONTENTS

CONTENTS

INTRODUCTION

Dear Reader,

"In the future, everyone will become world-famous for fifteen minutes," declared Andy Warhol, avant-garde artist and one of the 101 famous Americans portrayed here. Although Warhol's statement may be an exaggeration, it is true that we are living in what might be termed "the age of the celebrity." Magazines like *People* and *Fame,* and television programs such as "Entertainment Tonight" and celebrity talk shows, testify to our curiosity about those living in the spotlight.

Throughout history certain individuals have captured our imaginations with their courage, their accomplishments, or merely the force of their personalities. In this book, which will introduce you to famous Americans from Pocahontas to Bill Cosby, you'll read about 101 people who can indeed be called "famous" and who have had great influence on the growth of our nation and our society.

Choosing from among the thousands of Americans who have become famous since European settlers first arrived on these shores was not an easy task. I did set up some basic guidelines: I knew that each person chosen should have made a distinct contribution to the development of his or her field of endeavor—politics, art and literature, science, sports, or industry. I also decided that, as much as possible, everyone included should have been born here or become U.S. citizens early in their lives. (Two striking exceptions: George Balanchine, who created the first school of

American ballet, and John Kenneth Galbraith, who published ground-breaking studies of twentieth-century American economics.)

After creating a first-draft list, I asked friends and family for their opinions. And opinions are what I got—with gusto. A dear friend told me that if the novelist William Faulkner were not included, my friend would never feel quite the same about me. A stronger sentiment was voiced by my otherwise amiable brother, who threatened to banish me from the family if baseball great Jackie Robinson were not highlighted. Since each made good cases for their entries, I took their advice. (For those of my associates who do not see their favorite Americans listed here, my apologies!)

After further honing the list, I brought a selection to my editor, who had her exceptions and preferences. Finally the 101 people portrayed in this book were chosen.

My purpose was to write the kinds of biographies that you would learn from and enjoy reading at the same time. I have included the major events and accomplishments in the lives of these people, but have also tried to include anecdotes and colorful facts that would make this book fun. The one thing I could not do was provide an in-depth analysis of each person. For example: Why did the poet Emily Dickinson choose to spend her whole life in solitude? How did physicist J. Robert Oppenheimer feel when he was denounced as a Communist? Did Robert Peary really discover the North Pole or did he fabricate evidence to perpetrate a hoax? What was the real story behind pilot Charles Lindbergh's World War II exploits? These are just a few of the questions the portraits I've written cannot address in depth, but hopefully they will inspire you to read more.

Go to your local bookstore or library, and you're sure to find a number of biographies from which to choose. Read more than one book or article to see how the "facts" of history change, both

INTRODUCTION

with time and through the eyes of different biographers. Learn about the people behind the scenes—individuals who never became "famous"—and the work they did that made it possible for these superstars to shine.

Each of these famous Americans has contributed to the way we live today. Each one can teach us something about inspiration, determination, and creativity. I hope you enjoy reading about their lives and accomplishments.

—Suzanne LeVert

MUHAMMAD ALI

PROFESSIONAL BOXER

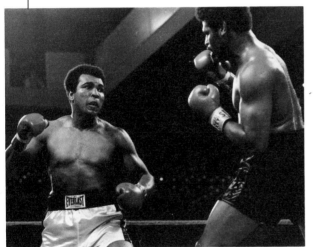

BORN *Louisville, Kentucky, January 18, 1942*

"**F**loat like a butterfly, sting like a bee." Those words describe perfectly the unique boxing style of Muhammad Ali, considered one of the finest boxers of the twentieth century.

"The Greatest," as he proudly calls himself, was born Cassius Marcellus Clay, Jr., in Louisville, Kentucky. His father was a sign painter, while his mother worked as a maid whenever the family needed extra money. The whole Clay family was expected to help out. When Ali was old enough, he took on a part-time job as a custodian at a nearby college.

Muhammad Ali about to deliver a powerful right cross to Leon Spinks

Strangely enough, Ali's boxing career began because his bicycle was stolen and he went to a police officer to report it. He was just twelve years old when the officer talked him into taking boxing lessons with other neighborhood kids at the Columbus Gym in Louisville.

His famous style, unequaled in the sport, developed in those early years. The champion himself later described it this way: "I learned there is a science to making your opponent wear down. I learned to put my head within hitting range, force my opponent to throw blows, then lean back and away. . . . When his best combinations hit nothing but air, it saps him." That technique, plus the famous footwork known as the "Ali Shuffle," brought him to the forefront of his sport.

After an impressive career as an amateur, winning two national Golden Gloves championships, winning 100 out of 108 fights and an Olympic gold medal, Ali turned professional in the fall of 1960. His trainer, Angelo Dundee, told *Time* magazine that he knew right away that Ali was a winner. "Not only did he have the talent, but he had the will. He ran eleven miles to the gym from the hotel and back every day. He was always the first in and the last out of the gym. . . ." He won his first pro fight on October 29, 1960—by 1963 he had fought nineteen pro fights and won them all. Then in February 1964 he went for the heavyweight championship against Sonny Liston and won the title in the seventh round in Lewiston, Maine. He would go on to win it twice more, for a record three times.

Almost as much as for his boxing finesse, Ali is known for his public persona—brash, confident, and controversial. During his boxing career, he used a showman's strategy for gaining public attention while intimidating his opponents. Spouting off poems in which he predicted the exact round of his opponent's defeat was just one well-known stunt.

But it was his joining of the Black Muslims, an Islamic black religious group, in 1964 that attracted worldwide attention from the general public. Changing his name from Cassius Clay to Muhammad Ali for religious reasons, Ali became an outspoken advocate for his religion.

In 1967 he was drafted into the United States Army during the Vietnam War. In keeping with Black Muslim teaching, he refused to serve. He was arrested and the World Boxing Association (WBA) stripped him of his heavyweight title and took away his license to box. Ali became a hero of the time, as supporters of the civil rights and peace movements admired his professional and personal sacrifices for the cause of peace. The U.S. Supreme Court later reversed his conviction and affirmed his conscientious objection to the war.

When the WBA returned his license in 1970, Ali went back to fight for his title. He hadn't lost his touch. After a few tough fights, he finally beat George Foreman in 1974, knocking him out in the eighth round in Zaire. Ali was able to defend his title despite failing health, until Larry Holmes defeated him in 1980.

Now retired from boxing, Ali spends his time making business investments and working for the Black Muslims. He remains in the eyes of the world one of "the Greatest" that ever was.

3

WOODY ALLEN

FILMMAKER

BORN *Brooklyn, New York, December 1, 1935*

Allen Stewart Konigsberg, born in Brooklyn, New York, in 1935, has made some twenty-three films over which he has had almost total artistic control. Given the freedom to choose his script, cast, production crew, and cinematographers, Woody Allen is one of America's only true "auteurs"—a filmmaker with a distinct, personal style and remarkable gift of creative and comic genius.

Woody, the son of Martin and Nettie Konigsberg, grew up in the Flatbush section of Brooklyn. A loner as a child, Woody loved

Woody Allen and Diane Keaton in Annie Hall

baseball, radio shows, and comic books. He also had a passion for comedy, especially the vaudeville routines that were still being staged at the Flatbush Theater. By the time he was fifteen, he was writing quips and one-liners of his own and sending them to newspaper columnists. A mention of his name in one of those columns led to his first professional job, writing one-liners for a press agent's clients.

After graduating from Midwood High School in Brooklyn, Woody attended New York University for one year before dropping out. He then started writing jokes and skits for television comedy shows and performers like Garry Moore and Sid Caesar, but never wanted to perform himself. His friends and fans finally forced him onstage, and it was in New York's Greenwich Village nightclubs that Woody Allen's comic persona was first born.

Woody's comic personality as a little man up against the complexities of the modern world comes through in all of his films. He is smart, but not physically strong or classically handsome. He is honest and bewildered at the moral corruption he sees around him. He's been bullied by "macho" men; he has difficult relationships with women. He's a lovable klutz, clumsy and self-conscious, and he makes us laugh while exploring some of the major themes of modern urban life—relationships, divorce, moral integrity, coping with the stresses of a fast-paced society. Even opening a box of frozen spinach is a hilarious adventure for Woody's character, as it was in *Bananas,* his second major film in 1971.

In nightclub routines, books, magazine articles, and especially in the twenty-three films Woody has made to date, this character has developed, as have Woody's talents as a filmmaker, writer, and actor. When we first meet him as Virgil Starkwell in *Take the Money and Run* (1969), he's a bungling amateur criminal. The film is almost all slapstick and sight gags—we laugh at what we see, not always what we feel about the character Woody

5

is portraying. But in later films we can see how Woody's comedy has developed.

In 1977, for example, in what some consider Woody's best film, *Annie Hall*, he plays Alvy Singer, a comedian struggling with questions about his creativity, the meaning of life and death, and his relationships with women. We laugh at what the character thinks about and the way he relates to the complex world around him, rather than at the things he does.

Woody does not star in all of his films, and not all of them have been comedies. As a filmmaker, he has grown from a slapstick comic to one of the most accomplished and respected American directors, winning two Academy Awards for Best Director and Best Screenplay for *Annie Hall* in 1977 and eight other nominations for directing and screenwriting.

Extremely private about his personal life, Woody is reported to be an intense and rather modest man. Known for his love of New York City, he frequently is seen walking the streets of Manhattan, playing the clarinet at Michael's Pub, or eating at Elaine's, a fashionable restaurant. Married and divorced twice, he is now living with actress Mia Farrow, with whom he has made four of his latest films. His first child, Satchel, was born in 1988.

SUSAN B. ANTHONY

SUFFRAGIST

BORN *Adams, Massachusetts, February 15, 1820*

DIED *Rochester, New York, March 13, 1906*

Susan B. Anthony lived in the 1800s, when women still wore constricting long skirts and painfully tight corsets. They frequently had restrictions placed on what they could do and say in public as well. They were given a minimal education and few choices about what kinds of lives they could lead. The participation of women in politics, for instance, was rare in this society. In fact, on one of Susan's earliest political outings, at a rally in favor of Prohibition (banning the sale of liquor), Susan was told that "the sisters [women] were not invited to speak, but only to listen and learn."

Susan would spend her life trying to lift women up from this oppression—to gain the right to vote, to receive equal pay for equal work, to be treated with dignity and respect, both in the workplace and at home.

Susan grew up in Massachusetts and New York, the second daughter of a Quaker, Daniel Anthony, and his wife Lucy. Daniel's ancestor John Anthony, Jr., had come to the New World from Hampstead, England, in 1634.

Susan most likely inherited her political instincts and indomitable spirit from her father. Daniel was a very righteous man, in favor of Prohibition and against slavery. He instilled his beliefs in his children and Susan was particularly affected. In addition, Daniel saw fit to give her an unusually good education, tutoring her and sending her to one of the few colleges that would accept women.

After her education was completed, Susan taught school, mainly to young women, in Pennsylvania and New York. Although she enjoyed teaching, the important issues of the day distracted her. She longed for a chance to participate and to make a difference in her society.

By this time, her family had moved to upstate New York, which became the birthplace of the women's rights movement. Elizabeth Cady Stanton, a leading suffragist (women's rights advocate), lived in the area at the time, and Susan took her place with Stanton at the forefront of the political arena. Susan and Elizabeth Stanton formed the Women's State Temperance Society of New York, an association in favor of Prohibition. This was one of the first organized women's political groups in the country.

When Susan tried to speak out in favor of Prohibition and against slavery, however, she realized that dignity and respect were being denied *her* simply because she was a woman. When she spoke at conventions, she was met with intolerance and prejudice from men—even men who were fighting for the same causes.

Susan realized that women would not be taken seriously until they had political power, and political power began with the right to vote—suffrage. Women's suffrage became Susan's abiding passion, and she pursued it from one end of the country to another. In state after state she challenged the laws denying women the right to vote on the basis of the Fourteenth Amendment to the Constitution, which provides equal protection under the law for all American citizens.

Susan dedicated her life to the cause of women's rights, frequently being arrested and harassed for her activities. When she died in 1906, she had seen women's suffrage granted in four states, but didn't live long enough to see it become a federal law in 1920. When we think of the incredible opportunities now open to women and the work still left to be done, we must thank Susan B. Anthony and the other notable women with whom she worked for laying a firm foundation.

LOUIS ARMSTRONG

JAZZ MUSICIAN AND COMPOSER

BORN *New Orleans, Louisiana, July 4, 1900*
DIED *New York, New York, July 6, 1971*

America's outstanding contribution to the art of music—jazz
—developed out of the unique experience of the black man in
America. One of the greatest jazz musicians in history was Louis
Armstrong who, with his raspy singing voice, mellow trumpet
playing, and generous spirit, brought to America and the world a
new appreciation of this music.

Louis' childhood was difficult. His family was desperately
poor, living for a time in a fifty-cent-a-month shack in the heart of
the black ghetto in New Orleans. The Armstrongs separated before Louis was five years old; he grew up without a father.

What might have become of him if he hadn't found music, we'll never know. Louis never received any formal education and spent most of his time in the streets of New Orleans. Luckily, he discovered his natural talent for music at a young age. By the time he was seven, he was singing in the streets for pennies to pay for food.

When Louis was thirteen, his street life caught up with him and authorities sent him to the Home for Colored Waifs for a year. There, Louis met Peter Davies, the home's bandmaster. He was given a bugle and taught to play. Louis absolutely fell in love with the instrument, learned to read music, and was soon leading the home's band.

When Louis was released, he had a new skill and a firm determination to pursue a musical career. He wasn't yet old enough to work in a band, but he hung around the honky-tonks and cafés, eager to listen and learn. He worked odd jobs to pay for the lessons he took from the King of Jazz himself, Joe "King" Oliver, the leading local musician.

When King Oliver left New Orleans for Chicago, he asked Louis to replace him in his band. It wasn't long before Louis began to shine—his golden tone and ability to improvise drew more and more people to hear him play.

According to some biographical sources, one of Louis' most important contributions to music was made by accident. One day, accidentally dropping his sheet music during a recording session, Louis began to improvise, using meaningless, but musically appropriate, sounds instead of words. This is called "scat" singing and other jazz greats, like Ella Fitzgerald and Joe Williams, are also known for their ability to scat-sing.

Soon Louis' singing was as popular as his trumpet playing. His talent for creating new musical forms expanded the standard Dixieland beat, in essence creating a whole new style of jazz.

In the 1930s, Louis began to play in front of big bands with forty or fifty instruments using popular songs rather than the blues numbers he had played with small bands of five or six players. The big-band "swing" era of the 1940s and Louis' influence upon it attracted millions of people to the world of jazz in all its forms.

It was while acting as a kind of goodwill ambassador of jazz that Louis truly thrived as a musician and a personality. The U.S. State Department sponsored him on many international tours, and his personal warmth won the hearts of Europeans and Africans alike.

Nicknamed "Satchmo" (a shortened version of "satchelmouth," used to describe his large lips and huge, puffed-out cheeks when he played his trumpet), Armstrong died in New York City on July 6, 1971, two days after his seventy-first birthday. He'll be remembered for his charm and wit, for his deep, compelling voice, and for his everlasting influence on American music.

NEIL ALDEN ARMSTRONG

ASTRONAUT

BORN *Wapakoneta, Ohio, August 5, 1930*

In 1986, Neil Alden Armstrong was named a member of the presidential commission to investigate the space shuttle *Challenger* disaster, in which six astronauts and one civilian were killed. A part of the space program since the earliest days of NASA (National Aeronautics and Space Administration), Neil Armstrong certainly had the qualifications needed to fill that post. Known best as the first man to walk on the moon, Armstrong's most important contribution to the program is his consistent pursuit of excellence and progress as a NASA astronaut and aerospace engineer.

Neil Armstrong (seated in front) during presidential commission's investigation of the space shuttle Challenger disaster

Born on his grandparents' farm in Ohio, Neil lived in six different towns—his father worked as an auditor of county records for the state of Ohio—before his family settled back in Wapakoneta when Neil was thirteen. Neil had a happy childhood and, though he was an excellent student and amateur musician, his overriding passion was always aviation. He took his first plane ride at the age of six, began to build model airplanes at nine, and took flying lessons at fourteen. On his sixteenth birthday he earned his pilot's license, even before learning to drive a car.

When he graduated from Wapakoneta High School in 1947, Neil entered Purdue University as a naval cadet to study aeronautical engineering, and won a Navy scholarship to pay for it. When he was called up for active duty two years later, he underwent flight training and was sent to Korea during the war. He returned a hero, having flown seventy-eight combat missions and winning three Air Medals. He then finished college, receiving a Bachelor of Science degree in 1955.

During the next seven years, Neil proved himself a most able and courageous pilot. Testing new planes for NACA (National Advisory Committee for Aeronautics, the agency that preceded NASA), he flew over 2,600 hours in various supersonic fighter and rocket planes. Then, in September of 1962, Neil was accepted into NASA's astronaut training program, fulfilling a lifelong dream of traveling in space.

After rigorous training, Neil was given command of the space vehicle that performed the first manual space docking maneuver in history, with *Gemini 8*, on March 16, 1966. On another mission, Neil was almost killed when he was forced to parachute to earth from 200 feet when the jet he was flying crashed.

NASA announced the crew of *Apollo 11*, designed to land men on the moon, on January 9, 1969. Neil was named along with Edwin Aldrin, Jr., and Michael Collins. These three men would take part in the most famous, and potentially dangerous, mission in the history of flight.

The *Apollo 11* space vehicle, assembled in a building fifty-two stories high at Cape Kennedy, Florida, lifted off at 9:32 A.M. on July 16, 1969. Less than twelve minutes after liftoff the vehicle went into earth orbit, and two and a half hours later it broke from the earth's gravitational pull and started its 238,857-mile journey to the moon.

Six and a half hours after landing, Neil emerged from the hatch of the landing module and stepped slowly down a ladder. As he did so, a television camera attached to the module transmitted his first step onto the powdery lunar surface to television viewers on earth. At that moment—10:56 P.M. on July 21, 1969—he uttered the statement that would go down in history: "That's one small step for a man, one giant leap for mankind." He and Edwin Aldrin spent some twenty-one hours on the moon, returning to earth with films and photographs and spectacular research material for geological studies, and information about how man reacted to the differences in gravitational forces that exist in space.

A very private and modest family man, Neil found the publicity before and after this incredible mission rather trying. Never a romantic about his role in the space program, he avoided, as best he could, the attention the first man on the moon would naturally attract. Since the *Apollo 11* mission, he has concentrated on furthering the aims of the space program. Leaving NASA in 1971 to teach aerospace engineering at the University of Cincinnati and work for private aerospace corporations, Neil remains dedicated to the U.S. space program today.

FRED ASTAIRE

DANCER, ACTOR

BORN *Omaha, Nebraska, May 10, 1899*

DIED *Los Angeles, California, June 22, 1987*

"I never thought a funny-looking guy like me would be suitable for pictures," Fred Astaire was once heard to remark. But this "funny-looking guy" was for millions of Americans the picture of elegance and the perfect dancer, lighting up the musical comedy stage and screen with his sparkling talent for nearly seventy years.

Combining tap, ballet, and ballroom dancing with a refined grace and charm, Fred has been called "the greatest dancer in the world" by many of his peers, including the late George Balan-

Fred Astaire and Ginger Rogers

chine, former director of the New York City Ballet, and Gene Kelly, a fellow musical comedy star.

Born in Omaha, Nebraska, in 1899. Fred first put on a pair of dancing shoes at age four, when his mother enrolled him in ballet class with his older sister, Adele, already a talented dancer at age six. A few years later the two youngsters were sent to study tap dancing in New York City.

Professional careers for the team began at ages twelve and fourteen, respectively. Playing in "every rat trap and chicken coop in the Midwest," Fred and Adele became one of the best-known dancers in vaudeville. They finally made it to the Broadway stage and stardom in 1917.

The Astaires starred together in some eleven musicals until Adele left the act to marry Lord Charles Cavendish, an English aristocrat, in 1932. A year later Fred fell in love himself and married Phyllis Potter, a wealthy and beautiful socialite to whom he was devoted. Fred then went to Hollywood for a chance to make it in the movie business.

"Can't sing. Can't act. Balding. Also dances." So read one Hollywood talent scout's assessment of Fred's potential. Despite this rather appalling description, Fred soon became one of RKO Studio's biggest money-makers and most beloved stars. His talent as a dancer and choreographer was complimented by a singing voice that brought the romantic lyrics of such illustrious songwriters and lyricists as Irving Berlin and Ira Gershwin to life.

Fred's elegance, on and off the screen, was countered by a down-to-earth, "everyman" kind of charm that endeared him to the movie-going public. Starring with some of Hollywood's most beautiful leading ladies, including Audrey Hepburn, Cyd Charisse, and Judy Garland, Fred made some thirty film musicals.

It is his partnership with Ginger Rogers, however, that is perhaps best remembered. Ginger's own extraordinary talent added an indefinable and unforgettable magic to Fred's choreog-

17

raphy. In such classics as *Top Hat*, *Swing Time*, and *Shall We Dance?* Fred and Ginger became the toast of Hollywood. In the splashy Fred-and-Ginger musicals, Americans in the depths of the Great Depression of the 1930s found romance, laughter, and hope. He continued to delight fans for years to come and received a special Academy Award in 1949 for his contributions to the cinema.

Although he made dancing look easy to audiences, he once told a reporter that "the only way I know to get a good show is to practice, sweat, rehearse, and worry." Indeed, Fred was a workaholic and a perfectionist, working up to eighteen hours a day for six weeks for each demanding role in a musical.

Fred also starred in dramatic films, displaying impressive acting ability. *On the Beach*, released in 1959, brought him critical acclaim, and he won an Oscar nomination for best supporting actor for *The Towering Inferno* in 1975. He made television specials, one of which, *An Evening with Fred Astaire*, won five Emmy Awards in 1958.

Fred continued to work well into his seventies, although he stopped dancing professionally in 1969. His wife Phyllis died in 1954, and he remained single until 1980, when he married Robyn Smith, a jockey with whom he shared a passion for horses. Fred died in Los Angeles of pneumonia in 1987, at the age of eighty-eight.

CRISPUS ATTUCKS

REVOLUTIONARY PATRIOT

BORN *Framingham, Massachusetts ? 1723 ?*

DIED *Boston, Massachusetts, March 5, 1770*

On March 5, 1770, Crispus Attucks was shot and killed by a British soldier in a riot that took place in Boston, Massachusetts —a riot known as the Boston Massacre. It marked the opening act of the American Revolution and Attucks, a runaway slave, was the first man to be killed.

Even today, not much is known about Crispus Attucks. Scant historical records indicate that he might have been born twenty-five miles west of Boston in Framingham, Massachusetts, then a farming community. His mother was a slave, and his father was most likely a native Indian of the Natick tribe.

Crispus Attucks (foreground) at the first battle of the American Revolution

We know nothing more about his childhood until he escaped from slavery on September 30, 1750, and his owner, William Brown, posted a reward for his return. Twenty-seven years old, six-two, and with short, curly hair, Crispus was worth just thirty British pounds, the equivalent of about ten dollars.

No one managed to capture him, however, and Crispus made his way to the Boston docks and was hired on a whaling ship. He worked as a seaman for nearly twenty years, until his ship came into port that fateful March day in 1770.

Boston was at that time an occupied town. British troops numbering over seven hundred had landed in full arms to protect the men who collected taxes for the King of England. "No taxation without representation" was a familiar refrain in Boston, and frequent demonstrations had erupted over the power the King exerted on the colonies' domestic affairs. When the troops arrived, the level of tension in Boston peaked.

According to some sources, what is often considered the opening salvo in the American Revolution started out in 1775 as a silly fight—this one between a barber's apprentice and a British soldier who, the apprentice claimed, had not paid the bill for his haircut. The apprentice accosted the soldier in front of the Customs House, where taxes were collected for shipment back to England.

When a British sentry intervened and pushed the apprentice down, cries rang out and a crowd gathered. A group of sailors led by a tall black man arrived, carrying sticks and rocks. The crowd hurled angry insults and comments at the sentry guarding his post.

If an order to fire was given, no one knows who gave it or when or why. But shots rang out—five men were fatally wounded and six others were injured. One of the dead was the black leader, Crispus Attucks.

Attention later focused on Crispus's actions. Some say he

20

struck the sentry with the stick he carried, others denied that any physical provocation had taken place. Some asserted that even if a stick had been raised, it had been in self-defense against a fully armed soldier.

And so our great fight for independence started with this incident, five years before the War of Independence officially began. How Crispus became involved that day, we'll never be sure. But his sacrifice must be remembered, and the freedom and liberty for which he died must remain a constant goal for every American.

JOHN JAMES AUDUBON

ORNITHOLOGIST, ARTIST

BORN *Les Cayes, Santo Domingo, April 26, 1785*

DIED *New York, New York, January 27, 1851*

Part businessman, part scoundrel, part naturalist, John James Audubon led a life that was as unpredictable as the wildlife he captured in his unique drawings. We know him best for his intricate paintings of birds published as a carefully researched catalog, *Birds of America*. The Audubon Society, named after him, is synonymous with conservation and ecology, and we look to it to help us protect our precious natural resources.

But the real John Audubon was far from the most devout naturalist, and his personality and life were far from serene and conventional. He was born to Jean Audubon, a French sea captain who was a prosperous trader in sugar, cotton, and slaves. Jean had many mistresses in various ports. One, a Creole woman known to history only as Mademoiselle Rabin, gave birth to John on the island of Santo Domingo. When his father returned to France, he took John and a daughter by another Creole woman back with him. The children were officially accepted by the Audubon family, including Jean's legal wife.

John, like his father, would lead an adventurous life. He was given a fine education, but had no real discipline or desire to learn about anything except drawing and nature, for which he had a great passion. At the age of eighteen, John left France for Philadelphia, near which his father had a small estate. Not exactly the picture of a rugged pioneer, he wandered about dressed in finery, honing his skills as a hunter and enjoying the American wilderness. His life as a country squire did not last long, however. Within a few years he lost the estate in a bad investment.

John, with no home and now married, decided to go West to make his fortune on the new frontier. But his business schemes fell through, one after another. Instead of selling to customers or tallying receipts, he would wander in the woods, hunting, fishing, and cavorting with the Indians. His family frequently had to live with friends as John constantly fought bankruptcy.

Finally accepting his failure as a businessman, he left his wife and children in Kentucky and embarked on an incredible journey across the United States. He decided, with customary vigor and self-importance, that he would draw and catalog each American bird, life size and in its natural surroundings. With gun, drawing paper, inks, and pencils, he traveled from state to state, stopping only to make money by painting portraits.

In all, he drew and described 489 different species of birds and established a reputation as one of America's finest ornithologists. Finally compiled, *Birds of America* spanned five volumes,

23

and its companion text, *Ornithological Biography,* another five. He later produced *Viviparous Quadrupeds of North America,* a stunning panorama of forest animals.

The legacy of Audubon's work must be judged in two different ways, as art and as science. While scientists find some of his paintings rather inaccurate and too "emotional," artists complain that he is too literal and his work too photographic. His written texts reveal a man not well schooled in grammar or spelling and with no real flair for language, and he had no formal scientific training. Most of the technical writing accompanying his drawings was done by others.

But his love for the wilderness and his excellent hand in capturing the magic world of birds have made Audubon's name synonymous with the responsibility each and every one of us has to the nature that surrounds us.

STEPHEN FULLER AUSTIN

FOUNDER OF TEXAS

B O R N *Wythe County, Virginia, November 3, 1793*

D I E D *Austin, Texas, December 27, 1836*

The great state of Texas contains approximately 267,339 square miles of America's richest, most fertile land. Absolutely stuffed with oil and natural gas, it is one of the country's leading energy providers. Cotton, wheat, corn, and rice all thrive in Texas soil, and only California surpasses Texas in the value of its agricultural resources.

Today there are over 16 million people who are proud to call themselves citizens of the Lone Star State. Its capital is Austin, a bustling, modern city named after the earliest American settler on Texas soil, Stephen Fuller Austin.

It was Stephen's father, Moses Austin, who first began the Austin legacy in Texas. After moving to the sparsely populated Missouri Territory from Virginia in 1798, Moses tried his hand at a number of trades among the mostly French and Spanish settlers. When those ventures failed, he obtained a land grant from the Spanish Government that had colonized much of the country of Mexico, including the huge Mexican region of Coahuila, and an area within it called Texas. When Moses died before the grant could be settled, twenty-seven-year-old Stephen stepped in. He would almost singlehandedly turn what was once an unimportant parcel of land into one of the greatest American states.

Many of the diverse occupations and interests Stephen had developed in his early years had trained him for such a venture. Living among Native Americans, Spanish, French, and adventurous Anglo-Americans in Missouri helped familiarize him with the delicate balance between these cultures that must exist for such a community to succeed. After receiving an excellent education at Yale College in Connecticut and Transylvania University in Kentucky, he returned to Missouri and took up a series of occupations. He became a storekeeper, manager of a lead mine, director of a bank, and a member of the territorial legislature. He was even appointed a judge when he moved to Arkansas, but probably never held court. Instead he decided to get some solid legal training by studying in New Orleans. He also worked at a Louisiana newspaper.

All of this experience, combined with his down-to-earth, kindly nature, and well-educated, clear thinking, made his role as founder of Texas that much more natural.

Within ten years, Austin had settled nearly one thousand new families onto Mexican soil, and obtained more and more land for new settlements. But his real importance lay in his dedication to not only populate the area, but to develop it as well. He mapped the province, promoted trade with the United States, and encouraged the establishment of schools and commercial industry. He worked to promote the rights of immigrants and homesteaders, and brought in a steady stream of new settlers. Texas became a thriving colony with a healthy economy and abundant resources.

It was Austin's delicate skills in diplomacy that allowed this development to take place. He was able to soothe the fears of the Mexican Government that Texas would be absorbed by the United States and, at the same time, calm the growing impatience of the settlers with the bungling of the new and still disorganized Mexican Government. Despite Stephen's best efforts and many years of negotiations, however, a bloody revolution took place and Texas was made part of the United States nine years after Stephen's own death. He died at the age of forty-three, two months after being named Secretary of State of the new independent Republic of Texas.

GEORGE BALANCHINE

CHOREOGRAPHER

B O R N *St. Petersburg, Russia, January 9, 1904*

D I E D *New York, New York, April 30, 1983*

The day George Balanchine died, Lincoln Kirstein, cofounder of the New York City Ballet, told an audience gathered to see a Balanchine work, "We know that this night George is probably teaching the angels to *tendu* [a ballet step]. The *angels,* who don't need to rehearse!"

George was a meticulous worker, a precise choreographer, and a creative genius. He was a hard-driving teacher, but one who had great love for his students and their capabilities. He inspired a great many of today's finest dancers.

To claim him as an American, however, is perhaps presumptuous. He was raised and trained in Russia from 1904 to 1921, and danced in Paris, Copenhagen, and London before arriving in the United States in 1933, when he was nearly thirty years old.

But George founded the first American ballet company, and from his efforts emerged a distinctly American style of dance. His enthusiasm and energy brought the dance into the hearts of many Americans for the first time, and his personal love for the artistic freedom he found in this country inspired him to become an American citizen.

Born Georgi Melitonovitch Balanchivadze in St. Petersburg (now Leningrad) Russia, he was the son of a composer. He was trained from the age of ten at Russia's famous Imperial School of Ballet, which graduated many other famous dancers. He himself graduated in 1921.

George left the Soviet Union forever in 1924 while on tour with the Soviet State Dancers, a ballet company, in Germany. Ordered to return to Moscow, he refused, instead going to Paris, where he joined the Ballet Russe, run by a fellow émigré, Serge Diaghilev. Diaghilev immediately saw Balanchine's immense talent as a creator of dances, and encouraged him to pursue a career as a choreographer.

George took his advice and had choreographed eight major dances before he reached the age of twenty-five. When Diaghilev died, George created several new ballets while working with various European companies, then presented his own dance company in Paris in 1933.

It was during this year that Lincoln Kirstein, a wealthy ballet enthusiast, invited Balanchine to America. It was Kirstein's hope that American-born and -trained dancers would someday compete artistically with their European counterparts, and he recognized in Balanchine the talent and energy to make that happen.

Together they created the School of American Ballet, the American Ballet Company, and a new performance company, the New York City Ballet, with Kirstein as general director and Balanchine as artistic director. In the nearly fifty years under Balanchine's tutelage, both the school and the company grew in prestige and popularity, as did Balanchine's reputation as a fine teacher and choreographer.

His unique style can be seen in each of his over two hundred ballets. Balanchine always emphasized the physicality of the dance—the precise yet graceful movements performed by carefully trained dancers. Costumes, decor, and even story lines were not as important; it was the finesse of the human body in movement that fascinated George and continues to delight his audiences.

His death at the age of seventy-nine was deeply felt by the dancers he had trained and the public he had entranced. Today the New York City Ballet continues to perform to sold-out houses in New York and around the world. The Balanchine tradition lives on under the leadership of his two most devoted disciples, Peter Martins and Jerome Robbins.

P. T. BARNUM

SHOWMAN

BORN *Bethel, Connecticut, July 5, 1810*

DIED *Bridgeport, Connecticut, April 7, 1891*

"There's a sucker born every minute" is a famous adage attributed to an equally famous man, P. T. Barnum. He made a fortune relying on his secure knowledge that every human being had a sincere desire to be fooled into believing what couldn't possibly be true!

Phineas Taylor Barnum was born in Bethel, Connecticut, the son of a hard-working farming family. He himself, however, had no intention of following in his father's footsteps, preferring instead to live off his wits in order to save strain on his muscles.

Hopping from one job to another—running an antislavery newspaper, selling theater tickets, working as a storekeeper—he couldn't seem to find his niche.

Until the day he met Joice Heth. It was through his experience with her that he realized that money and fame could be had by banking on the incredulity of the public. Joice was an aged black woman who claimed to be 161 years old. Barnum could see that she was a hoax, but he was convinced that a yellowed piece of paper—what appeared to be an original bill of sale from Washington's father—would be enough to fool a gullible audience.

Barnum saw his opportunity and snatched it: Joice, coached to remember all the details of Washington's youth, was marketed with industrious zeal. When she died, far too soon for P.T., he turned another trick. He wrote two sets of anonymous letters, one attacking Joice's authenticity and the other defending it, and had them published in a local newspaper. The controversy he created with this publicity stunt made his name into a household word.

P.T. made show business his life, and in 1841 acquired two "curiosity" museums in New York City. He merged the two to create the American Museum, a huge carnival of events, both bizarre and educational in nature. Alongside minerals, fossils, and natural history exhibits were curiosities and hoaxes, like the bearded lady (no lady at all!) and the Feejee Mermaid (actually the head and torso of a monkey sewn to the tail of a fish).

P.T.'s most famous drawing card was General Tom Thumb, an intelligent, engaging dwarf named Charles Sherwood Stratton. P.T. found him when the dwarf was just a boy and within a few years made him a giant of a celebrity, here in America and throughout the world.

We know P.T. best, perhaps, for his fabulous three-ring circus, which he first opened in Brooklyn, New York, on April 10, 1871, and called "the Greatest Show on Earth." There were trapeze artists, a menagerie of wild animals, curiosities like Tom

Thumb and the Feejee Mermaid, clowns, acrobats—all under one colorful roof. Every year throngs of children and the young at heart came to see his world-famous circus.

As P.T. grew older, younger, more energetic men tried to copy his circus. Deciding to beat them at their own game, he merged with his main rival, Londoner James Bailey, to create an even bigger extravaganza. The Barnum & Bailey Circus, now combined with the Ringling Brothers, provides the modern world with the joy and excitement P.T. had developed with such flair and style.

In many ways, P.T. himself was as much of a curiosity as his show. With ironic humor and a keen eye for a fast dollar, P.T. called himself the "Prince of Humbugs" and entertained millions with his exploits. When he became ill in his eighty-first year and realized he was dying, he arranged with a New York newspaper to print his obituary—two days before he died—so he could see what they said about him. It's doubtful he would have changed a word of it; he once said, "I don't care much what the papers say about me, provided they say something."

33

CLARA BARTON

HUMANITARIAN

BORN *North Oxford, Massachusetts, December 25, 1821*

DIED *Washington, D.C., April 12, 1912*

Every year thousands of Americans who are homeless and hurt from fires, floods, accidents, and war receive lifesaving care from the American Red Cross, a unique relief organization founded by Clarissa Harlowe Barton.

Clara was born in North Oxford, Massachusetts, the youngest daughter—by ten years—of a family of five children. Because of the difference in age between herself and her siblings, Clara was raised almost as an only child. As such, she became used to having things her own way. This sense of determination, coupled with a great deal of nervous energy, allowed her to pursue a rather unorthodox career.

At fifteen, she began teaching, a vocation she pursued for eighteen years. Teaching helped her overcome a shy and rather self-centered nature, and encouraged a clever mind. Unfortunately, "clever" women were not always appreciated in those times, and her industrious creativity met with much resistance.

In Bordertown, New Jersey, for instance, she introduced free education for all by converting the exclusive school into a free public school. She offered to serve without pay for three months if the townspeople made the school free for all children.

The experiment was a success. Under her direction the school more than tripled its enrollment and became a valued town institution. But, deciding that the powerful school Clara created should not be run by a mere woman, the town proceeded to demote her. Clara, enraged and unable to accept a subordinate position, quit. She never taught school again.

Her next job brought her to Washington, D.C., where she worked in the U.S. Patent Office. When the Civil War broke out, Clara heard stories of the incredible suffering of the soldiers at the front, and although neither a nurse nor formally trained in either medicine or business, she decided to help. She herself brought supplies to the front, distributed them, and even nursed the wounded. For this she became known as the "angel of the battlefield."

Exhausted after the war and suffering from nervous tension, she went to Europe to rest. Never one for sitting on the sidelines, even while recuperating, it wasn't long before she involved herself in another project. The Franco-Prussian War began in 1870 and Clara assisted the International Red Cross, organized in 1863, in distributing relief throughout Europe.

When Clara returned to the United States, she brought with her a strong determination to see her country become a part of

35

this great agency's efforts at home and abroad. Organized as a nonpartisan relief agency to aid those wounded or displaced by war, the International Red Cross also established the Geneva Treaty. This treaty, now ratified by the United Nations, "neutralized" any member of the Red Cross, allowing him or her to safely work in warring nations without regard to nationality or politics.

Back in the United States, Clara worked toward two goals: to have the United States sign the Geneva Treaty and to create the American Red Cross. Once again faced with a challenge, she worked tirelessly to resolve it.

Clara began a campaign of education, personally visiting heads of the State and War departments, influential members of Congress, and lawyers to encourage ratification of the treaty. To raise money for the American Red Cross, she distributed a pamphlet describing the organization and its purpose to the public at large, asking them for support. Finally, in 1881 the United States adopted the Geneva Treaty, and the next year Clara established the American Association of the Red Cross. She was its president for twenty-three years.

Administration was never her strong point, however, and she resigned from the presidency amid reports of mismanagement. But her devout patriotism and deep caring for others' suffering were qualities that set her apart and are carried on today by noble Red Cross volunteers around the world.

ALEXANDER GRAHAM BELL

INVENTOR, SCIENTIST

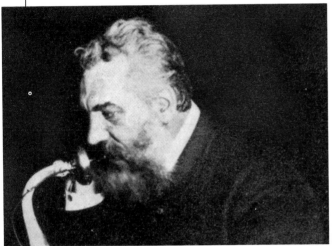

BORN *Edinburgh, Scotland, March 3, 1847*

DIED *Cape Breton Island, Nova Scotia, August 2, 1922*

United States Patent number 174,465—it would be hard to imagine modern life without the invention this patent protects. Day-to-day life as we know it would be completely altered and certainly much quieter, for Patent number 174,465 was issued for the invention of the telephone, the greatest single contribution to the art of communication since the pencil.

The man responsible for the sound of ringing bells and dial tones is Alexander Graham Bell, a man who, ironically, dedicated a great deal of his life to helping and understanding the deaf. It was, in fact, through his studies of sounds as they relate to the human ear that the principles behind a working telephone were revealed to him.

Both his father, Alexander Melville Bell, and his grandfather, Alexander Bell, were deeply involved in the science of speech. Alexander would follow in their footsteps, expanding upon their work.

Alexander was a particularly brilliant and precocious young man. He received his education in Scotland and was graduated from the Royal High School in Edinburgh at the age of thirteen. By the time he was just sixteen, he was already teaching elocution and music at the Weston House Academy and taking graduate-level courses at the University of Edinburgh. When his grandfather died in 1865, he became his father's assistant in London. It was through his work there that his interest in helping the deaf became a lifelong commitment.

In the early 1870s Alexander taught Visible Speech, one of his father's techniques for teaching the deaf, at the Boston School for Deaf Mutes (later the Horace Mann School). After that, he became a professor at Boston University as well as continuing to take on private pupils. One of these students, Mabel Hubbard, herself deaf from the age of five, would become his wife and devoted helpmate.

Alexander began to concentrate on expanding his knowledge of the underlying principles of sound reproduction. Specifically, he related those principles to the telegraph, an invention recently improved upon by fellow inventor Thomas Edison, from Samuel Morse's original creation. Not long after Alexander arrived in America in 1870, he began experiments to see if he could invent a telegraph machine that would transmit more than one message at a time—by using vibrations of different pitches. These experiments led to the first American patents granted to him.

It was the idea of a speaking telephone that occupied much

of his scientific efforts, however. Applying what he had learned from his work, both with the telegraph and with the human ear, he realized that any sound—including the human voice—could be reproduced using wires and receivers similar to those used in the telegraph. After much experimentation, the first telephone transmitted its first intelligible sentence, six historic words spoken by Bell to his assistant, Tom Watson: "Watson, come here. I want you."

Alexander went on to make further improvements in the electrical reproduction of sound, not only on the telephone but on another famous invention of Edison's, the phonograph. His work with the deaf never ceased.

In his later years he studied aviation, and his work in that field laid the basis for many aspects of modern aerodynamics. He worked on the newspaper *Science* with his father-in-law, Gardiner Hubbard, and from 1898 to 1904 he was president of the National Geographic Society.

His achievements and awards were many, and one of those he most cherished was the granting of American citizenship in 1882. He died in Nova Scotia at the age of seventy-six. He was buried on his estate, in a tomb cut into rock on the top of a mountain. At the time of the burial, telephone service throughout the United States was discontinued for one minute—a fitting tribute for a great scientist and humanitarian.

39

LEONARD
BERNSTEIN

CONDUCTOR, COMPOSER

BORN *Lawrence, Massachusetts, August 25, 1918*

A musical Renaissance man with unique style and energy, Leonard Bernstein is the first musical conductor of international stature to be born and trained in the United States. He has made classical music accessible and fun for children and adults more than anyone else in American history. He has composed some of our best-loved musicals as well as first-rate operas, ballets and symphonies. He is not only a conductor of world renown, but a virtuoso pianist as well.

Leonard discovered his love and talent for music when he

was just ten years old. His parents, both Russian immigrants, were rather surprised when their son, who had spent most of his youth outdoors playing baseball, began playing an old upright piano stored in their basement. At this early age, Leonard already had a musical career as his goal and spent every spare moment practicing.

His enthusiasm was matched by extraordinary talent. By the age of fourteen, he'd learned all that local instructors could teach him and went to Boston for further study. He then studied composition and piano at Harvard University after graduating from the Boston Latin High School. His next stop was the esteemed Curtis Institute in Philadelphia where he studied conducting.

The music world began to notice this brash young man after he published his first significant piece, the Clarinet Sonata of 1942, and produced operas for the Boston University of Modern Art. When he was appointed assistant to Serge Koussevitzky, one of this century's most important conductors, at the Berkshire Music Center in Tanglewood, Massachusetts, his future looked bright indeed.

In 1943, Leonard was appointed assistant conductor of the prestigious New York Philharmonic. Then, on November 13, at the last minute and with no prior rehearsal, Leonard replaced guest conductor Bruno Walter. Leonard's impromptu debut stunned the audience and critics alike and brought him to the attention of the international music-loving public. After his New York triumph, he appeared as guest conductor for many major American and European orchestras. In 1958 he became conductor of the New York Philharmonic and has remained affiliated with it as laureate conductor since 1969. He has also conducted the Israel Philharmonic on numerous occasions.

Leonard is especially noted for his deeply moving renditions of the works of Gustav Mahler, Ludwig von Beethoven, and American composers. His own compositions range from classical

41

to show tunes, often winning high critical praise and enjoying widespread popular appeal.

Almost as much as his musical style, however, it is Leonard's personal flair that makes his influence felt so strongly. His energy, both conducting and lecturing, is known to be contagious —his audiences leave his presence with a new appreciation of music.

When he brought his love for music to the television screen in the Young People's Concerts, he also brought a deeper understanding of serious music to children and music lovers of all ages. In these concerts, he conducted the orchestra, interrupting frequently to lecture about the music his audience was hearing.

Although now retired from full-time conducting to spend more time composing, Leonard can be found back at the podium ready to conduct with his usual flair and vigor on special occasions, such as the spectacular Bicentennial tour in 1976. There were numerous celebrations during 1988 in honor of his seventieth birthday. As his operas, symphonies, musicals, and televised lectures continue to be repeated, American music will be influenced by his unique style for generations to come.

ELIZABETH BLACKWELL

PHYSICIAN

B O R N *Bristol, England, February 3, 1821*

D I E D *Hastings, England, May 31, 1910*

In 1857 the New York Infirmary and College for Women, under the leadership of Dr. Elizabeth Blackwell, first opened its doors. It was a historic moment, for this hospital was the very first of its kind—all of its administrators and doctors were women. For the first time, female patients received medical attention from doctors of their own sex and female physicians had a place to train and work.

Elizabeth Blackwell was an extremely determined young woman. She grew up in a family of hard-working achievers, and in the Blackwell home unconventional behavior was the rule. Her mother was a highly cultured woman who imparted a love for art and music to her children. Both she and Elizabeth's father believed that all of their nine children, including their five daughters, should have the opportunity to fulfill their intellectual potential. The Blackwell family moved to New York from England in 1832; then, hoping to better their financial situation, they moved to Cincinnati. Three months later Mr. Blackwell died, leaving his family destitute.

To support themselves, the Blackwells opened a school, the Cincinnati English and French Academy for Young Ladies. Elizabeth, however, never really enjoyed teaching. She was far more interested in the social issues of the day, especially abolition and women's rights. She watched with envy the activism of her two younger brothers, Samuel and Henry, political reformers who were married to suffragists.

According to many biographies, it was as she cared for a sick friend, dying of a gynecological disease, that Elizabeth's true vocation was revealed to her. After discovering the kind of care her friend was receiving from unconcerned and insensitive male doctors, Elizabeth realized that her friend might have been spared much of her suffering had a female doctor cared for her. It was then that she decided to become a physician herself.

She found two doctors, Samuel Dickson and her brother John, to tutor her, and she continued to teach in order to pay for her studies. In 1847, she applied to a dozen medical colleges—and all rejected her. Finally, the administrators at a tiny college in upstate New York (now Hobart College) presented her case to its students for a vote. Mainly out of curiosity, the all-male student body voted to admit her.

Elizabeth worked hard, fighting against prejudice and cynicism from both her classmates and the faculty. But her perseverance and the honest delight she took in her work won most of them over, earning their personal respect and professional admiration. In 1849 she became the first woman ever to graduate from a certified American medical school.

Elizabeth's career in medicine centered around her deep concern about the lack of attention paid to hygiene and sanitation as factors in the spread of disease. In particular, she focused on sexually transmitted diseases and women's vulnerability to them. These concerns formed the cornerstone of both her political philosophy and her medical practice.

After opening the New York Infirmary and later (in 1865) setting up the Women's Medical College associated with it, Elizabeth decided to leave both in the very capable hands of her younger sister, Emily, who had also become a doctor, and another colleague, Sister Mary Zakrzewska. Elizabeth left New York for England, where she suffered from poor health for the remainder of her life. Until her death in 1910, she continued to practice and teach medicine when she could, and encouraged other women to follow her path. Her legacy to the thousands of women now part of the medical profession is incalculable.

45

DANIEL BOONE

FRONTIERSMAN

BORN *Reading, Pennsylvania, November 2, 1734*
DIED *St. Charles County, Missouri, September 26, 1820*

W as Daniel Boone a remarkably fearless pioneer or just one of many men who searched for a new life in the West? Was he, as John James Audubon once described him, "gigantic"? Or was he "common," as the editor of the *Missouri Gazette* saw him?

Many details of Daniel's life are obscured, either by a lack of facts or pure exaggeration, but we do know that he was an accomplished frontiersman. He learned the crafts of weaving and black-smithing from his parents, Squire and Sarah Morgan Boone, and at the age of twelve had become an expert hunter and trapper. By the time the Boone family moved west to North Carolina in 1750, Daniel had developed quite a love for the wilderness. While he worked for his father as a blacksmith, he spent every spare moment honing his skills as a woodsman and marksman.

Daniel also had a passion for excitement, which eventually took him far from home into the thick of a perilous military battle. Accompanying British General Edward Braddock during the French and Indian Wars, he took part in the disastrous fight to take Fort Duquesne from the French in 1755. On July 9 over nine hundred French and Indian soldiers set upon Braddock's army. Over half of Braddock's men were killed, while the others, including Daniel, narrowly escaped by horseback through the treacherous woods. Daniel made his way back to North Carolina and his father's farm. He met and married Rebeccah Bryan a short time later.

Never content to stay at home for long, Daniel set out once again for Kentucky, then a large expanse of unsettled land west of the Allegheny Mountains. Populated by Indians, it possessed rich natural resources. Daniel's adventures on these trips are largely undocumented, but we know that he was captured by Indians on at least two occasions but always managed to escape.

In 1775 he became an agent of Richard Henderson's famous Transylvania Company, an ambitious association formed to colonize what is now Kentucky and Tennessee. It was Daniel himself who took the first division of pioneers into the territory. The settlement they formed was called Boonesborough, after the brave man who cleared the land for it. A small enclave of families, including Boone's own, lived inside a sturdy fort built largely by Boone's own labor.

Daniel spent the next few years protecting the fort against Indian attacks and hunting, fishing, and trapping for the pioneers. He also surveyed the land for new settlements and mapped out the region's rivers, streams, and trails.

By this time, Kentucky had been organized as a county of Virginia, and Daniel was made captain of its militia, officially giving him the responsibility he had taken upon himself naturally. In the years that followed, Daniel continued to explore the territory and was appointed to a number of different government positions, all the while accumulating new parcels of land for settlements.

After spending his entire life clearing land for a growing America, his land claims were declared invalid when Kentucky became an independent state, no longer bound by territorial agreements. He left the state and joined his son, who had inherited a pioneering spirit from his father, in West Virginia. A few years later they moved to settle in the Missouri territories.

Although the last few years of Daniel's life were spent haggling over property rights with the United States Government, his rank in American frontier history has never been disputed. Known for his courage and personal integrity, he remains one of our nation's most respected and beloved heroes.

KIT
CARSON

FRONTIERSMAN, SOLDIER

BORN *Madison County, Kentucky, December 24, 1809*

DIED *Fort Lyon, Colorado, May 23, 1868*

"**D**ear old Kit . . . O wise of counsel, strong of frame, brave of heart and gentle of nature . . ." Spoken by a close comrade at the time of his death, those words correctly characterize this great adventurer.

In frontier history, it could be said that where Daniel Boone left off, Christopher "Kit" Carson took up. He was born in a town not far from Boonesborough, Kentucky, in 1809 where his parents, Lindsay and Rebecca, had traveled from North Carolina. Like Boone, Carson had a pioneering spirit, and when his mother tried to apprentice him to a saddle maker, he would have no part of such an ordinary occupation. Instead, he ran away and joined a caravan expedition to Sante Fe, New Mexico, when he was sixteen.

Kit never had any formal schooling, and would remain illiterate until the last five or six years of his life. But instead of "book learning," he was educated in the fine skills of hunting and trapping. In a way, then, this first expedition west served as Kit's high school education, for he returned home one of the most adept woodsmen and mountain climbers in the country.

These skills served him well, especially after he met up with Lieutenant John Charles Frémont, known as the Pathfinder. A celebrated explorer, Frémont led a famous expedition through California to acquire it from Mexico. When Frémont's memoirs were published, Kit's role in this expedition was highlighted and he became known throughout America as a brave, loyal, and clever frontiersman.

During his many adventures, Kit became acquainted with Native Americans from many different tribes. He met them not only as enemies on the battlefield, but also as friends in the new frontier. He took the time to learn about their culture and understand their customs. He even served as a United States Government agent for the Ute tribe in Colorado, working to negotiate treaties between the two parties. He fell in love and married an Arapaho woman who bore him a child. Later, when this woman died, Kit brought his daughter back east to be raised by his relatives.

However, his personal empathy for the Indian culture and cause did not stop him from becoming one of the most adept Indian fighters in the West. At first he felt unable to fight against people he felt were being wronged by the United States Government. But the war between the white man and the Indian was a complicated one. Kit found himself torn between the righteousness of the Indian's position and the fact that many innocent pioneer families were being brutally killed by Indians.

Kit decided to fight, and the Apaches, the Comanches, the Kiowas, and especially the Navahos became his enemies. In one campaign he forced some eight thousand Navahos to surrender. Despite their devastating defeat, Kit earned their respect as a worthy warrior.

In 1867, Kit was again made an Indian agent for the United States Government. He was respected for his integrity by both the Indians and the government. As one fellow mountain man once said, "Kit Carson's word was as sure as the sun comin' up."

Kit lived the last few years of his life in poor health and in pain from a tumor pressing against his throat. He died on May 23, 1868, after living one of the most exciting and adventurous lives in American frontier history.

RACHEL CARSON

ENVIRONMENTALIST, AUTHOR

B O R N *Springdale, Pennsylvania, May 27, 1907*

D I E D *Silver Spring, Maryland, April 14, 1964*

❝The beauty of the living world I was trying to save has always been uppermost in my mind," wrote Rachel Carson about her book, *Silent Spring.* With this poetic, yet scientific book, published in 1962, the fate of the earth's resources became a real issue to many Americans for the first time. As one editorial put it, "A few thousand words from Rachel Carson and the world took a new direction."

Rachel grew up learning to appreciate the natural world, inheriting her mother's love for books. Rachel had her first story published when she was just ten years old, and always knew that she would be a writer someday.

After being accepted to Pennsylvania College for Women, Rachel studied English until her third year. Then she made a decision that completely changed her life. A required course in biology so intrigued her that she changed her major to science.

Although professional female scientists were quite rare at that time, Rachel was both determined and brilliant. After graduating magna cum laude, she was awarded a scholarship to the world-renowned Johns Hopkins University in Baltimore, Maryland. There she studied zoology, genetics, and biology with some of the world's finest professors. Even before receiving her master's degree, she began teaching at both Johns Hopkins and the University of Maryland.

Rachel had to leave the academic life after her father died in 1935 to help support her widowed mother. After working some thirteen years as an aquatic biologist at the U.S. Bureau of Fisheries and Wildlife, she became editor-in-chief of their publications department. Here, Rachel helped promote the agency's objective: "to insure the conservation of the nation's wild birds, mammals, fishes and other forms of wildlife."

In addition to her work at Fisheries and Wildlife, she began to publish articles on wildlife and ecology in magazines and journals. Attracting national attention, she published her first full-length book, *Under the Sea-Wind: A Naturalist's Picture of Ocean Life.* This book was highly acclaimed, both for its scientific content and its unusually poetic and accessible style. A second work, *The Sea Around Us,* was reviewed with equal enthusiasm.

In the late 1950s, Rachel became concerned about the use of chemicals to kill insects—such chemicals are known as insecticides. One particularly deadly chemical, DDT, was then in widespread use. DDT was first used to kill disease-causing mosquitoes and insects harmful to agricultural crops. It was soon discovered that DDT also destroyed birds, plants, and harmless insects.

Rachel began to imagine what the world would be like if we continued to use these killer chemicals—no birds, no fish, no cattle, in essence, a barren planet. Gathering evidence from scientists in America and Europe, and drawing upon her own vast knowledge, she wrote *Silent Spring,* which warned against the dangers of the irresponsible use of chemicals.

Although *Silent Spring* was critically acclaimed, both for its literary style and meticulous research, it was denounced by the agricultural chemical industry and some of her scientific colleagues as being too "emotional." Many felt that the benefits of insecticides outweighed the harm they caused the environment. This debate continues to rage today.

Rachel produced this book at great personal cost. Her health had been failing; she suffered from arthritis and was stricken with bone cancer. Confined to a wheelchair and in pain, she still managed to testify before Congress and played an important role in making laws to protect the environment. She died in 1964.

54

GEORGE WASHINGTON CARVER

AGRICULTURAL CHEMIST

BORN *Diamond Grove, Missouri, c. 1861*

DIED *Tuskegee, Alabama, January 5, 1943*

Born a slave in rural Missouri at the start of the Civil War, George Washington Carver grew up to become a national symbol of achievement. After centuries of slavery, blacks lacked practical skills and were routinely denied the opportunity to learn them. George worked to help make life better for his people.

As a child, George was owned by a middle-aged couple, Moses and Susan Carver. George and his older brother Jim lived with the Carvers, even after their mother was kidnapped and killed by a bounty hunter. The Carvers treated them like members of their family.

George Washington Carver talking with an ROTC student at Tuskegee Institute

George was a sickly child and remained frail all his life. He stayed inside, helping with the housework, learning to knit, sew, and care for plants so well that he was known in the neighborhood as "the plant doctor." He would use all those skills throughout his life, frequently paying for his education by taking in laundry and sewing.

George stayed with the Carvers until he discovered that the local school would not admit blacks and left home in search of an education. Finally, ten years after leaving home, he graduated from high school in Minneapolis, Kansas. Accepted into Highland College in September 1885, he arrived on campus only to be turned away. The college had not known he was black.

Still hoping to get a college degree, he moved east to Iowa, where he managed to secure a place at a local school, Simpson College. He studied painting here, then went on to study horticulture at the Iowa State College of Agriculture, where he was the first black ever to be admitted.

He experienced humiliating discrimination, was forced to eat in the basement with the field hands, and was denied a place to live until one of the professors gave up his office so George could sleep there. But he persevered, holding back anger and quietly moving ahead. He did well in his classes, received a bachelor of science degree in 1894, and a master's degree in 1896.

It was his deep commitment to bettering the lot of the newly freed black man that led him to join up with Booker T. Washington at the Tuskegee Institute. Here blacks were given practical, industrial training so they could attain economic independence. Booker and George hoped that by competing with whites on equal terms, blacks could break down the barriers that separated the races.

As director of the agriculture department at Tuskegee, George focused on ways to make farming easier, more profitable, and less taxing on both the backs of the farm workers and the land itself. Cotton, the south's biggest crop, depleted the soil and was difficult to grow and maintain. Instead of depending on that crop, George felt that others, such as cow peas and sweet potatoes, could be more versatile and less harsh on the land. Peanuts and soybeans were especially soil-enriching, and it was his experiments with them that made him famous. He concocted over three hundred products, from cheese and milk to coffee and facial cream—all out of peanuts! Unfortunately, many of them proved too difficult or expensive to produce and were therefore impractical for widespread use.

History places George in a curious position. While his accomplishments were indeed significant for a black man at that time, his passiveness toward the racism aimed against him and his people was seen as submission by many blacks. He made influential white friends, but remained almost subservient to white people he didn't know. He never expressed outrage or anger against racism.

His greatest achievement, then, was in what he symbolized to blacks and whites alike—the chance for a black man to get ahead, despite seemingly insurmountable odds.   57

CÉSAR CHÁVEZ

LABOR ORGANIZER

BORN *Yuma, Arizona, March 31, 1927*

César Chávez, now president of one of the largest unions in America, grew up poor and hungry, working the lush farmlands of California. César and his family were migrant workers—they traveled from farm to farm, state to state, living in makeshift shacks, going hungry, barely eking out a living picking grapes, lettuce, and other crops for as little as fifty cents a day.

By the time César dropped out of school in the seventh grade, he had attended more than thirty grammar schools in his twelve short years. Like thousands of others, César spent his childhood in frustration, unable to get a decent education and discriminated against because he was Mexican-American.

Despite his lack of education, César was a bright and perceptive boy. He was twelve when he first came into contact with a union, the Congress of Industrial Organizations (CIO), and realized that unions represented a way to fight the agricultural business that took such advantage of its workers. By joining together in a union, workers could have power over their employers. If demands for better wages and working conditions were not met, they could go on strike until their employers were willing to bargain with them.

Except for a year-long stint in the Navy, César worked in the fields until he took a job with the Community Service Organization, a local California agency set up to help migrant workers with day-to-day problems. He worked for them for many years until, in 1962, he left the organization to organize farm workers into a union.

At first many of the people he dealt with, both in the city government and in the fields, dismissed him as being "just a kid" because of his boyish looks and lack of confidence. But he soon developed a compelling personal style. His soft-spoken but mesmerizing voice and generous manner evoked dedication and trust in a rapidly growing number of followers. His firsthand experience of the migrant farming lifestyle made him different from many of the other labor organizers, who were generally college-educated men and women from big cities like New York or Los Angeles. He wore jeans and flannel shirts instead of suits, and went from door to door talking with each worker personally.

Because of the migrant nature of farm labor and the fact that many farm workers are in the United States illegally from Mexico, the Philippines, and elsewhere, unionizing this industry was, and continues to be, a difficult task.

In 1965 César and members of an organization he helped to

59

found, the National Farm Workers Association (NFW), joined a group of eight hundred migrant Filipino grape pickers striking against the grape growers for higher wages. Knowing that his relatively small union was not strong enough to withstand a long strike, he asked for and received support from other, more established unions and civil rights groups around the country. Then, by merging with a part of the American Federation of Labor–Congress of Industrial Organizations (AFL-CIO), he transformed a small organization into the United Farm Workers union (UFW), now a powerful national entity.

When the strike entered its second year, César reached out to the public at large, all across America, for additional moral and financial help. To attract attention to his cause, he used some rather untraditional methods, like conducting church meetings, holding sing-ins, and going on long marches. A devout Catholic, César deeply believes in nonviolence, and his methods reflect this belief.

By the end of 1968, millions of people had been persuaded by César's compelling message not to buy table grapes from growers who would not bargain with the UFW. This strategy, called a boycott, cost the grape industry 20 percent of its market in 1968. Two years later César and the UFW finally won their fight.

César went on to lead the UFW in a number of successful battles, including a lettuce boycott in the mid-1970s. César remains deeply devoted to the union cause. Today another boycott against table grapes is being waged by César and the UFW to protest the use of certain pesticides considered dangerous to the grape pickers. With immigration laws a major issue and with the Midwest farming community suffering a devastating economic crisis, César has many more challenges to face.

SAMUEL LANGHORNE CLEMENS (MARK TWAIN)

AUTHOR, HUMORIST

BORN *Florida, Missouri, November 30, 1835*

DIED *Redding, Connecticut, April 21, 1910*

Two of the most unforgettable characters in American literature, Tom Sawyer and Huck Finn, were created by one man—a man whose life was as filled with adventure as his stories and novels. Samuel Langhorne Clemens, also known as Mark Twain, wrote in a distinctly American voice, filled with humor, irony, and sympathy for the unique characters he drew.

Samuel's parents, John and Jane, moved their family to the small town of Hannibal, Missouri, on the banks of the Mississippi River in 1839. John, a shopkeeper, always believed that his risky land investments would someday make him rich. Although he did in fact own a valuable piece of property, the Clemenses lived in relative poverty. When John died in 1847, his six children had to leave school to help support themselves. Samuel was just twelve years old.

Sam worked as an apprentice printer on his brother's small newspaper in Hannibal, then took his new trade on the road, working as a printer for newspapers in St. Louis, Philadelphia, and New York. In 1857, Sam returned to Missouri and embarked on a four-year career as a steamboat pilot on the mighty Mississippi. Later calling this period the most gratifying in his life, Sam wrote that the Mississippi was his "brief, sharp schooling in human nature."

The Civil War signaled another exciting period in Sam's life. After serving in the Confederate Army for a short time, he made his way to Nevada, where his brother Orion had been appointed to the territorial government. After a brief and financially disastrous stint as a silver prospector, Sam wisely decided to return to writing.

62   Taking a job at the *Territorial Enterprise*, a Nevada newspaper, Samuel began his career as a journalist in full. It was here that Sam began to use his pen name, Mark Twain, for the first time. A term used by Mississippi boatmen to indicate water two fathoms deep, the name Mark Twain quickly became identified throughout the world with humorous, insightful writing.

Sam spent the rest of his long life with pen in hand. As a journalist for various newspapers, he traveled extensively in the United States, Europe, and the exotic islands of the Pacific. He also lectured on a regular basis, especially when various business investments left him short of cash.

We know him best, however, for his many short stories and novels. Drawing upon his experiences in Hannibal, in the Civil War, in Europe and Hawaii, Sam described the people he met and

housing project. His comedy career started in elementary school, where he performed impromptu routines for his classmates. While he would have the class roaring with laughter, his clowning would cause him more than a little trouble. Bill never was interested in his studies, and left school after he was informed he'd have to repeat the tenth grade.

It wasn't until he'd spent four years in the Navy that he realized the importance of education and learning. As he told a reporter for *Senior Scholastic* magazine in 1965, "I met a lot of guys in the Navy who didn't have as much 'upstairs' as I did—yet there they were, struggling away for an education. I finally realized I was committing a sin—a *mental* sin." He studied for and passed a high school equivalency exam, then went on to study physical education at Temple University on a track-and-field scholarship. Education remains a top priority for Bill.

After performing at a small club in Philadelphia when he was a sophomore in college, however, Bill knew that he belonged in show business. Starting out performing improvisations and jokes in coffee houses and nightclubs in Philadelphia for as little as five dollars a night, he made a quick rise to stardom. In just three years he was so popular and in so much demand that he made $7,000 per college concert and $25,000 a week at Las Vegas nightclubs.

Bill Cosby's humor frequently focuses on his childhood, especially his rivalry with his two younger brothers, Russell and Robert, and on observations about everyday life that diverse audiences can relate to and laugh at. He has made over twenty comedy albums to date, almost all selling over a million copies each, and has won eight Grammy awards.

His career in television is no less impressive. He was the first black actor to star in a weekly TV series when "I Spy" was put on the air in 1965. He won three Emmys for his portrayal of Alexander Scott, a debonair CIA agent. Bill played opposite

65

Robert Culp, and the easy friendship and equality between the two characters, one black and one white, represented a true step forward for race relations on television.

When "I Spy" went off the air in 1969, Bill concentrated more time on his family, his education, and his comedy. He made movies in Hollywood, like *Uptown Saturday Night* and *Let's Do It Again*, both with Sidney Poitier; he also continued to make comedy albums and perform his stand-up routine in nightclubs. Another television series, called the "Bill Cosby Show," ran for nearly two years and a number of television specials kept Bill in the spotlight throughout the 1970s.

Bill was committed to bringing "The Cosby Show" to America even before it was put on the air on September 20, 1984. Strange as it may seem today, he had a hard time selling the idea for the show to the networks. He was told by executives that sitcoms were dead and that shows depicting black families were even harder to sell. But Bill pressed the issue and finally NBC took a chance. "The Cosby Show" has been a hit right from the start, with no end of its success in sight for the show or for the star who brings it so much life.

Bill's commitment to education, especially for black Americans, remains firm. Most recently, he made one of the largest individual gifts ever made to a black educational institution, Spelman College in Georgia. He also is the author of two bestselling books, *Fatherhood* and *Time Flies*.

66

WALTER CRONKITE

JOURNALIST, ANCHORMAN

BORN *St. Joseph, Missouri, November 4, 1916*

"And that's the way it is," a voice rich with authority would tell Americans every night at the end of the "CBS Evening News." The voice belonged to a man who, for over forty years as an anchorman and reporter, gave us our good news and bad—wars, presidential elections, successful and unsuccessful space missions, famous weddings, and natural disasters. Walter Cronkite has won countless awards for journalistic excellence and is considered America's finest broadcast journalist.

Walter knew he wanted to be a reporter ever since he read a

short story about a foreign correspondent in the magazine *American Boy*. He put those dreams into action when he became the editor of his high school's yearbook and newspaper. At the University of Texas, where his father taught dentistry, Walter studied political science, economics, and journalism, and obtained some hands-on experience working for the *Houston Post* as a campus reporter.

Dropping out of college in his junior year, Walter began his professional career as a reporter and radio announcer. When World War II broke out, he was sent overseas as a United Press correspondent, earning international recognition for his coverage of major battles. When the war ended, Walter covered the trials of Nazi war criminals in Nuremberg and was the bureau chief of United Press in Moscow. Then, in 1948, he took a job back in the United States as a Washington reporter and broadcaster for a group of Midwestern radio stations.

In 1950 he joined the news department at Columbia Broadcasting System and a great partnership was formed. Regularly appearing on public affairs programs and news shows, Walter remained dedicated to news reporting. In 1952, Walter covered the first nationally televised presidential nominating convention and then hosted all election night television coverage by CBS until he retired in March 1981.

We know him best, however, in his role as anchorman, reporter, and editor for the "CBS Evening News." *Time* magazine described him as "the single most convincing and authoritative figure in television news," and millions of Americans relied on Walter to bring them the news every night. Known for his objective, clear, and direct reporting, Walter infrequently revealed his biases and true feelings.

His famous eyebrows, however, raised and lowered in subtle, perhaps unconscious expressions of opinion, sometimes gave him away. As he once told a reporter, "It's a difficult thing in televi-

68

sion to keep one's facial expression from betraying prejudice, bias, or attitude on a story. One doesn't want to be a mask, an automaton." Walter realized that television could change the way Americans felt about the world by physically showing them what they once could only hear about or read. The events of the world now came into their living rooms, in sometimes graphic detail— soldiers in war, politicians on the campaign trail, death, and corruption. Walter was careful not to abuse the power of the medium and his role in it.

Despite his frantically busy schedule as anchorman and editor at CBS, Walter never stopped writing many of his stories, editing all of them and doing much investigative reporting. His coverage of the Vietnam War in the 1960s and 1970s was especially important, as he was one of the first reporters on a major network to declare the war unwinnable.

Since his retirement as anchorman in 1981, Walter has kept his hand in the broadcast world by producing occasional news documentaries on a variety of subjects. In 1984, he accompanied President Reagan on his historic visit to the beaches of Normandy, forty years after the D day invasion. Now one of America's most respected political figures, Walter's precise, well-trained journalistic eye has inspired the trust of three generations of Americans.

CLARENCE DARROW

LAWYER

BORN *Near Kinsman, Ohio, April 18, 1857*
DIED *Chicago, Illinois, March 13, 1938*

"I speak for the poor, for the weak, for the weary, for that long line of men who, in darkness and despair, have borne the labors of the human race." Charles Seward Darrow, born into a poor family near a small Ohio town, became one of this country's preeminent attorneys, trying some of the most important legal and social cases in American history.

Clarence grew up in Kinsman, Ohio, the son of Amerus and Emily Darrow. Both his parents were intelligent, compassionate people who instilled a love for knowledge and literature in their children from a very young age. Both Amerus and Emily were involved in social reform, particularly women's suffrage (right to vote) and black emancipation. Their liberal opinions put them at odds with their more politically conservative community, and the resulting feeling of alienation was something Clarence would carry with him throughout his life.

Despite the intellectual atmosphere present in the Darrow household, Clarence developed an early love for just plain fun and an extravagant sense of humor. Baseball was an abiding passion, and later poker would serve as a diversion from his tiring work as an attorney.

Clarence entered college at the age of sixteen. After a year he began teaching elementary school in Kinsman when a financial setback in the family made it impossible for him to continue his education. It was during this period that he decided to become a lawyer. Later he joked that he chose law "to avoid hard work," but between his law practice, lecture tours, and writing commitments, Clarence Darrow was one of the busiest men in the nation.

Clarence discovered early in his career that he not only had a keen legal mind, but also an impressive speaking voice. After he and his first wife, Jessie, moved to Chicago to set up his practice, Clarence began speaking at Democratic political rallies, surprised at his ability to sway crowds. He also loved to write, not only legal briefs and political articles, but short stories and novels.

All of Clarence's talents would be called upon in a career that would crisscross with some of the most momentous events in the nineteenth and twentieth century. The labor movement, in its efforts to unionize, called upon Clarence's remarkable powers of persuasion to put their demands across. Defending Big Bill Haywood, a Western Federation of Miners leader, in one trial, and members of the United Mine Workers and International Workers

71

of the World organizations in many others, Clarence became the voice of labor during this particularly difficult time in labor history.

Then, in 1924, he was again thrust into the national spotlight when he defended two young men, Nathan Leopold and Richard Loeb, who confessed to kidnapping and murdering a fourteen-year-old boy. In this landmark case, Clarence used psychiatric evidence to defend his clients against the death penalty. He convinced the jury of their insanity, and Leopold and Loeb were sentenced to life imprisonment instead of the death penalty.

Clarence Darrow tried hundreds of cases—for labor, for the right of free speech, and against capital punishment. But the trial for which he is best known, nicknamed "the Monkey Trial," made national headlines once again. In Dayton, Tennessee, Clarence successfully defended the right of a high school teacher to teach the theory of evolution in his science classes.

Clarence Darrow tried most of his cases for little or no money. He and his second wife, Ruby, (he and Jessie were divorced) lived modestly in Chicago between bouts of poverty and international fame. Clarence remained an ardent supporter of social and racial equality, and spent his life trying to educate the public on these issues. He died in Chicago at the age of eighty.

EUGENE V. DEBS

LABOR LEADER

BORN *Terre Haute, Indiana, November 5, 1855*

DIED *Elmhurst, Illinois, October 20, 1926*

"**Y**ou should know that your sons were meant to be more than fodder for cannons." For saying these words with the United States on the brink of World War I, labor leader Eugene Debs was sentenced to ten years in jail as a traitor under the Espionage Act. Although his imprisonment might be considered unconstitutional now, Eugene Debs suffered his sentence with dignity as the father of the American labor movement, until he was pardoned a few years later.

Eugene was born into a large, affectionate family of French

immigrants; his father worked as a manual laborer and grocer to make ends meet. At the age of fifteen, Eugene dropped out of school to work as a railroad fireman.

It was in this job that Eugene was first exposed to labor unions and the desperate need for them. Many of the things we now take for granted, like health insurance and unemployment compensation, did not exist then. Working conditions were dangerous and employees were underpaid. Debs saw that workers had no power against the huge railroad companies—unless they joined together in a union. Throwing his whole heart into the labor movement, he helped organize a local chapter of the Brotherhood of Locomotive Firemen.

Eugene felt that all railroad workers should organize into one union, instead of separating into different ones according to particular jobs. Toward this end, he helped form the American Railway Union and was elected its first president.

Although rarely anxious to call for strikes, conditions were worsening for workers, and Eugene led his union out on strike against the Great Northern Railroad in 1894. Within three weeks, the railroad gave in and more workers flocked to join the union.

Another strike, against the Pullman Company, caused the U.S. Government to react with fury. Many American leaders still considered unions to be dangerous. President Grover Cleveland ordered federal troops out to suppress the strike. Within a few months nearly a hundred civilians had been killed or wounded during the demonstrations. Eugene himself was arrested and jailed.

Thanks to help from lawyer Clarence Darrow, Eugene only spent six months in jail. But while in jail he read many socialist writers and grew to believe that socialism was the only way to win justice for the working man.

Touring the country by train, this tall, bald man gave endless speeches for unions and socialism, shaking a long, bony finger at the crowd. As the leader of the Socialist Party of America, he brought in almost a million votes in the 1912 election—almost 6 percent of the national vote, more than any other third party up to that time.

A committed pacifist, Eugene opposed American entry into World War I. When the country was drawn into the war in 1917 and 1918, Congress and President Woodrow Wilson passed harsh laws against dissenters. Like Eugene, many Americans were imprisoned then simply for saying what they thought, without ever advocating or committing a violent act. Few people, however, received such a harsh sentence—ten years in jail, for a man who was 63 when he went to prison.

After two and a half years, Eugene's health had deteriorated to such a degree that the government pardoned him. He was still popular, having run for President from his jail cell and receiving nearly one million votes. After his release, he pressed for prison reform and continued to write about political issues, but never regained his strength. He spent much of his last few years in hospitals.

Since his death, many of the reforms which he fought so hard for have been adopted—unemployment and health insurance among others—making life better for the average American working man and woman.

75

EMILY DICKINSON

POET

BORN *Amherst, Massachusetts, December 10, 1830*

DIED *Amherst, Massachusetts, May 15, 1886*

"**I** am . . . small, like the wren, and my hair is bold like the chestnut burr, and my eyes, like the sherry in the glass that the guest leaves." So the solitary poet Emily Dickinson described herself in a letter to a friend in the mid-1880s. Such a description is very helpful, for not many people saw Emily Dickinson. She spent nearly thirty years almost completely alone—seeing no one but family members and a very few close friends. Her rather sad, hermitlike existence casts a shadow of mystery over the five volumes of exquisite, refined poetry she wrote.

Emily was born into a fairly wealthy, highly intellectual family in Amherst, Massachusetts. Her father, Edward, was a leading lawyer and politician who served as the treasurer at Amherst College, which his father had founded. Emily Norcross, her mother, was sickly most of her life, needing constant attention from Emily and other family members.

Emily received a more formal and extensive education than most women of her time. She studied in public schools until she enrolled at Amherst Academy, a private preparatory school, then went on to South Hadley Female Seminary, (now Mount Holyoke Academy). Among her friends, she was known for her lively wit and sense of fun. She loved music and frequently took part in dances organized by her friends. She flirted with her older brother's college friends, sending comic valentines and innocent notes.

It wasn't until Emily was in her early twenties that her more quiet, introspective nature began to dominate her personality. The occasional solitary walks she took as a teenager were conducted more and more often; she became impatient with her family's many social obligations. Her shyness, which had seemed charming to many new acquaintances, had become an extreme fear of strangers.

Why Emily's personality developed in this way is still unclear. Some historians speculate that a tragic love affair, either with a man her father did not approve of or someone already married, sent Emily into hiding. Others believe that Emily suffered from a psychological disorder, and still others think she felt stifled by the lack of social opportunities open to women at the time. Instead of fighting for an equal place in society, Emily might have chosen to retreat behind closed doors.

For whatever reasons, Emily lived in her family's house for her entire life, almost never leaving home. Her days were spent caring for her parents until they died and tending to housekeeping and gardening.

Emily Dickinson's life, therefore, was a life of the mind. Her greatness lies not in her day-to-day activities, but in what she imagined and was able to write down. She was dedicated to expressing in words the depth of emotion that she could not, or would not, express verbally.

With guidance and encouragement from her mentor, editor Thomas Wentworth Higginson, with whom she corresponded, Emily revealed her genius for the demanding art of poetry.

From 1858 until her death in 1886, Emily spent much of her time huddled over a writing desk. Each poem was carefully conceived, flowing from her heart but written with exacting concern for form, meter, and tone. On her death, at age fifty-five, Emily had written over 1,500 short poems, many of them classics, to be treasured by generations of readers.

WALT
DISNEY

MOTION PICTURE PRODUCER

BORN *Chicago, Illinois, December 5, 1901*
DIED *Los Angeles, California, December 15, 1966*

When Walt Disney received the U.S. Presidential Medal of Freedom, it was as an "artist and impresario [who] in the course of entertaining an age . . . created an American folklore." Walt Disney's unique vision, technical skill, and dedication to quality and excellence have made childhood memories of Mickey Mouse, Donald Duck, and Snow White—memories that last throughout our lives.

Walt was the youngest of five children born to Elias and Flora Disney. It was at the family farm, in Marceline, Missouri, where they moved shortly after Walt was born, that he first started to draw. His first subjects were the farm animals that he grew to love until the Disneys left rural life for Kansas City when Walt was eight years old.

Walt, always an industrious student, also worked hard as a newspaper delivery boy to earn and save money. He made his start as a professional artist at age sixteen, making a sketch every week for a local barber, who paid him twenty-five cents or gave him a free haircut.

After studying photography and drawing in high school and at the Chicago Academy of Fine Arts, Walt discovered his true vocation while working as a cartoonist for a small Kansas City newspaper. When he later did some work for a film company, he realized the amazing potential of merging the two mediums. Filmed cartoons—animation—became his passion.

Walt joined his brother, Roy, in Los Angeles, and together, with very little money, they formed their own film studio. It is said that Walt came up with the idea for his best-loved character, Mickey Mouse, while on a train trip from New York to Los Angeles. A rough draft was finished before Walt reached L.A., and in just a few months he and Roy had perfected the little mouse in a short film called *Steamboat Willie*—the first Disney film to include a soundtrack. Hundreds of cartoons featuring Mickey, Donald Duck, and other characters were produced by the Disney brothers and their employees in the years that followed.

Walt's company, Walt Disney Productions, Ltd., grew rapidly, and so did his experiments in film and popular entertainment. *Snow White and the Seven Dwarfs,* released in 1937, was the first feature-length cartoon in history. He followed it with other gems, like *Pinocchio, Bambi, Dumbo, Legend of Sleepy Hollow,* and *Wind in the Willows.* Walt personally took great care with the work produced at his studio, even after he no longer drew each character himself.

The golden age of animated Disney films in the 1930s and 1940s gave way to live-action dramas and comedy films for television and general cinema release. A weekly series—best known as "The Wonderful World of Disney,"—became a tradition for millions of American families. Some of Walt's most celebrated work during this period consisted of his nature documentaries. Walt's films have won an astounding twenty-nine Academy Awards.

Perhaps his greatest achievement—Disneyland—opened in 1955 in Anaheim, California. A huge amusement park, jam-packed with adventurous rides and intricately designed nature exhibits, Disneyland and its later Orlando, Florida, counterparts, Disney World and Epcot Center, represent the fulfillment of Walt's dream to bring magic into our lives. Roving life-size Disney characters—such as Mickey Mouse, Donald Duck, Pluto, Goofy, and Snow White—welcome millions of Americans to these fun parks every year.

Today, over twenty years after Walt's death, Disney Productions has experienced an exciting rejuvenation, releasing some of our favorite movies, like *Outrageous Fortune* and *The Flight of the Navigator*. The Disney Sunday Movie and a Disney cable TV network continue to entertain children of all ages and keep Walt's legacy alive.

FREDERICK DOUGLASS

ABOLITIONIST, ORATOR

BORN *Tuckahoe, Maryland, February (?) 1817*

DIED *Washington, D.C. February 20, 1895*

At the age of eight, Frederick Douglass learned "the secret of the white man's power to enslave the black man." That secret was education and knowledge, which most white men denied black men for as long as they could. Frederick learned to read only because the woman who owned him had a merciful streak. Once the secret was revealed to Frederick, he did everything in his power to be free, and to free others from the chains of slavery. Against remarkable odds, Frederick Douglass became one of the nineteenth century's greatest orators and a leader in the struggle for civil rights.

Born Frederick Augustus Washington Bailey to a slave, Harriet Bailey, and an unknown white man, Frederick was taken from his family to a plantation twelve miles away. Frequently hungry and without enough warm clothing in winter, Frederick suffered the humiliation and degradation of slave life as best he could. He worked both in the fields and as a house slave in Baltimore, where he first realized that freedom was possible, if only in the pages of a book.

When he was sent back to toil once again in the fields, he did so knowing that he had to escape to freedom in the North. When he was approximately sixteen, he made his first attempt, but was captured and jailed until his master sent him back to Baltimore. While being trained in ship repair, Frederick made another escape, this one successful. He made his way to New York City and from there sent for Anna Murray, a free black woman he had met and fallen in love with in Baltimore. They were married and moved to New Bedford, Massachusetts.

Although he was not enslaved in the North, Frederick still found there was a great deal of prejudice against black men and women. He found it necessary to change his name to avoid capture, and while he was well spoken and educated in a trade, he was unable to find a job with white men. His wife worked as a housekeeper and he as a common laborer for over three years.

In 1841, Frederick attended a convention of the New England Anti-Slavery Society, an abolitionist group headed by William Lloyd Garrison, a progressive white man. There, Frederick was urged by a friend to address the conference. Although he stammered a bit at first, his eloquence and passion affected the whole crowd. Garrison, convinced that Frederick could speak out against slavery with a unique authority, hired him on the spot as a full-time lecturer for the Society.

Thrust into national prominence, Frederick became a major spokesman for abolition. Unlike some of his fellow blacks, who

83

were embittered and angry, Frederick urged nonviolence and hoped for peaceful change. This position put him at odds with some of his own people, but helped him win the favor of many white abolitionists, thereby putting him in a position of relative power in the North. He founded the newspaper *North Star,* in which he expressed his admiration for the American ideal of democracy. He asked not for changes in the basic system, but demanded that the rights guaranteed in the Constitution be given to every man, woman, and child in the United States.

As time passed, however, Frederick realized that the American economy was too dependent on slavery for it to be dismantled without a fight. The winds of war were blowing throughout the United States, and although the reasons for the Civil War were complex, Frederick took the opportunity to help make slavery a major issue. He worked to allow black men to fight for the Union cause. Nearly 200,000 blacks fought and helped bring the North to victory.

After the Civil War, Frederick became an important voice during the period of the Reconstruction. He was also an outspoken proponent of equal rights for women and worked with leading suffragists for both the female and black vote.

Frederick's last years were spent in comfort and honor. He held a number of positions in the U.S. Government, including marshal of the District of Columbia and consul general to the Caribbean nation of Haiti. He wrote profusely and as eloquently as he spoke. He died suddenly, at the age of seventy-eight, at his home, Cedar Hills in Washington, D.C.

84

BOB
DYLAN

FOLKSINGER, COMPOSER

<u>**BORN**</u> *Duluth, Minnesota, May 24, 1941*

"**Y**ou don't have to starve to be a good artist. You just have to have love, insight and a strong point of view." Coming to prominence as a spokesman for the protest movement of the 1960s, Bob Dylan has been singing to America for over twenty-five years.

Born Robert Zimmerman in Duluth, Minnesota, Bob was the older of two children born to Abe and Ruth Zimmerman. When he was just a baby, his family moved to the nearby town of Hibbing. Bob grew up there, watching as the once prosperous mining town slipped into the decline that engulfed so much of the industrial Midwest. It was here that he experienced firsthand many of the themes he would sing about during his musical career.

Bob discovered his love for music at a very young age. He taught himself guitar by the age of ten; by fifteen he had mastered piano and harmonica, and had begun composing his own music and writing lyrics.

The protest folk music of the 1930s heavily influenced Bob's musical development, especially the songs of Woody Guthrie. In addition to making him more aware of the poverty around him in his own town, Guthrie's songs about the hobo lifestyle of the poor man in search of work also inspired a wanderlust in Bob. From the age of ten until he left for good at eighteen, Bob ran away from home seven times.

After receiving his high school diploma and a scholarship to the University of Minnesota, he began his college career, which lasted only six months before he again decided to make another trip across America.

When Bob made his way to the coffeehouses of Greenwich Village in New York City in the early 1960s, he found an eager audience for his songs depicting the despair of the poor and the horrors of racism. Always tinged with urgency and compassion, and frequently with cynicism and humor, songs like "Blowin' in the Wind" and "The Times They are A'Changin' " were the banners of a generation. What he wrote in the 1960s both reflected and inspired a whole movement, mainly among young people, aimed at changing American values and politics.

As the movement for change grew, so did Dylan's popularity. From performing for fifty or a hundred fans in a small cafe to singing for thousands at peace rallies and concerts, Bob became a superstar. Although forever linked with the protest movement of the 1960s, Bob has never let the urgency of his message get in the way of his creative genius. When he introduced a full electric blues-rock accompaniment into his act at the Newport Folk Festival in 1965, he singlehandedly presaged Bruce Springsteen, Bob Seger, and others by inventing what has become known as folk rock.

In the summer of 1966, Bob broke his neck in a motorcycle accident, forcing him to take a long rest from public performances. He reemerged a few years later to attract new fans with his music, now thoroughly infused with rock and roll, blues, and jazz, as well as folk rhythms.

In the late 1970s, Bob experienced a religious awakening, and many of his later compositions have a religious as well as political message. His activism has remained as alive as his creativity. Most recently, Bob took part in Live Aid and Farm Aid, large concerts for which he and other superstars donated time and talent to raise money for those in need in Ethiopia and the American farm belt.

AMELIA EARHART

AVIATOR

BORN *Atchison, Kansas, July 24, 1897*
DIED *Somewhere in the South Pacific, on or about July 2, 1937*

"Women must try to do things as men have tried. When they fail, their failure must be but a challenge to others." A woman ahead of her time, aviator Amelia Earhart lived a short life of accomplishment and adventure, and the mystery that surrounds her death sometimes overshadows the enormous contributions she made to twentieth-century aviation.

Even as a young girl, Amelia showed courage and imagination, despite a difficult childhood. Known for her love of the outdoors, Amelia also was rather clever with her hands. At the age of eight, she built a working roller coaster in her backyard.

Although her father, Edwin, was a kind man, he suffered from alcoholism, causing the family to live in constant social peril. The Earharts moved from town to town in the Midwest and Amelia's education was frequently interrupted. In 1914, Amelia's mother took her two daughters to Chicago, where they finished high school two years later.

In December of 1917 Amelia left a small community college in Pennsylvania to visit her sister, who was studying in Toronto, Canada. Impulsively Amelia decided to stay on, nursing soldiers wounded in World War I. The daring exploits of the dashing Royal Flying Corps ignited Amelia's first desire to fly.

At the same time, her experience tending the soldiers sparked an interest in medicine. With help from her parents, she enrolled in Columbia University's School of Medicine in New York. Despite her fine academic abilities, however, Amelia's heart was never in her studies. She would eventually receive a teaching degree, but becoming a pilot was her only real ambition.

The year after aviator Charles Lindbergh made his famous transatlantic flight, Amelia Earhart would become equally famous —as the first female *passenger* to cross the Atlantic in 1928—as part of a publicity stunt sponsored by a wealthy socialite and publisher, George Putnam. Although Amelia never touched the controls, she kept the log of the trip and was greeted as a heroine upon her return—complete with ticker-tape parades in New York and Boston.

But that was just the beginning. After marrying George Putnam, Amelia finally received her pilot's license and began a breathtaking series of aeronautical feats, remarkable even today. In 1932, she became the first woman to fly a plane alone across the Atlantic; in 1935, she made the first solo flight from Honolulu to the American mainland; she was also the first person to fly nonstop from Mexico City to Newark, New Jersey.

One of her proudest achievements, however, was her appointment in 1935 to Purdue University as a career counselor for women aviation students. Long frustrated by the lack of encouragement given to women in the male-dominated field of aviation, Amelia was pleased to give other women the advice they needed to become pilots, too.

Amelia was anxious to pilot "just one more long flight." In order to study human reactions and mechanical performance at high altitudes and extreme temperatures, Amelia's last flight was supposed to take her around the world.

Amelia and her navigator, Fred Noonan, left Miami, Florida, on June 1, 1937. They stopped in Puerto Rico, Venezuela, Brazil, and New Guinea. Then, during the most difficult leg over the Pacific, there was trouble. On July 2 at eight forty-five, they radioed that the plane was losing fuel. And that was the last time their whereabouts were known.

Neither Amelia, Fred, nor the plane was ever recovered, despite extensive searching. In one of Amelia's letters, written during the trip and "to be opened only in case of death," Amelia wrote a line that sums up her courageous spirit: "Hooray for the last grand adventure. I wish I had won but it was worthwhile anyway . . ."

MARY BAKER EDDY

RELIGIOUS LEADER

BORN *Bow, New Hampshire, July 16, 1821*

DIED *Chestnut Hill, Massachusetts, December 3, 1910*

Christian Science, a religion born out of one woman's struggle to find peace and freedom from pain and illness, now has a
worldwide membership of over 175,000 (according to a recent
estimate by the *New York Times*). The Church of Christ, Scientist
is headquartered in Boston, Massachusetts, and sponsors reading
rooms and churches throughout the United States and around the
world.

The woman responsible for creating this new religion was
Mary Baker, born in New Hampshire in the early 1800s. The

youngest of six children, Mary had a childhood marked by illness, with both physical and psychological symptoms. Although no doctor ever diagnosed a specific disease, she was subject to seizures and hallucinations all her life.

Because of her poor health, Mary's education suffered. Unable to attend school, she developed a lifelong love for literature but was educated in little else, other than religion. The Bakers were stern New England Protestants, and religious training was an important part of their daily routine.

Though at one time a member of the Tilton Congregational Church, Mary's spiritual needs were not met. Instead she took to her bed until she was twenty-two, when she married the first of three husbands, George Washington Glover, in Charleston, South Carolina. After only a few months Glover died of fever, leaving Mary alone, destitute, and pregnant. With the aid of local charities she was returned home to New Hampshire, where she gave birth to her only child, George.

Living at her parents' home, Mary had a series of nervous seizures and collapses. Because she was unable to care for her child, he was placed in the custody of one of Mary's former nurses and moved to another town. She would remain in contact with George but would never again live with him.

In 1853 Mary married Dr. Daniel Patterson, a dentist who traveled from town to town to treat patients. Mary moved with him to several small towns in New Hampshire, where they lived for nine years in relative poverty. When Patterson was taken prisoner by the Confederates during the Civil War, Mary moved into her sister Abigail's home. Now a complete invalid, Mary was sent to a sanitorium for intensive care.

Two months later, still suffering, Mary decided to visit Dr. Phineas Parkhurst Quimby of Portland, Maine, a spiritual healer. Quimby believed that one person could relieve a sufferer's symptoms by the power of strong, positive thoughts and the laying of hands on the sufferer's scalp.

When Quimby treated Mary, the results were startling. For the first time in her life, she began to feel and appear healthier. Mary stayed with Quimby for several weeks, learning his methods and philosophy. One of Quimby's ideas struck her most particularly: that disease was both caused and cured by the powers of the mind—in effect, that illness was merely a physical manifestation of one's own belief.

In 1866 Quimby died, and a month later Mary apparently injured her spine in a fall. Told by doctors that she would never walk again, and unable to find a Quimby disciple to help her, Mary cured herself by taking up the New Testament of the Bible. In it, she found another link to spiritual healing—her faith in Jesus Christ. It was then that she decided she had a divine responsibility to bring her methods of spiritual healing to the rest of the world.

After divorcing her second husband, Mary concentrated on writing *Science and Health,* a book published in 1875 that describes in detail her philosophy. Her third husband, Asa Gilbert Eddy, helped her found and fund the First Church of Christ, Scientist in Lynn, Massachusetts in 1879. It would later move to Boston. By 1906, there were over 85,000 Christian Scientists.

93

The last decades of Mary's life were shrouded in mystery. Retiring in 1889 to Concord, New Hampshire, she returned to Boston just four times, leaving the administration of the Church to her assistants. She did, however, found *The Christian Science Monitor* two years before she died. First published to address the bad publicity the Christian Science Church was receiving, the *Monitor* today has an outstanding reputation for international coverage of political and social, as well as religious, news reporting. Mary Baker Eddy died at the age of eighty-nine.

THOMAS ALVA EDISON

SCIENTIST, INVENTOR

BORN *Milan, Ohio, February 11, 1847*

DIED *West Orange, New Jersey, October 18, 1931*

Thomas Alva Edison, now regarded as a central figure in the technological revolution of the twentieth century, began his career selling newspapers and candy on a train in Michigan. He had almost no formal education and very little money, but he did have plenty of imagination and determination. Setting up a chemistry lab in the train's baggage car, Tom worked on his first inventions.

Tom was the youngest son of Nancy and Samuel Edison, owner of a lumberyard and shingle mill in the canal town of Port Huron, Michigan. Tom spent the earliest part of his childhood getting into mischief, but suffered a nearly fatal bout of scarlet fever when he was seven. It is believed that this illness affected his hearing, for Tom was somewhat deaf for the rest of his life. In childhood, this deafness contributed to the growing solitary side of his personality—he took long walks alone and spent endless hours poring over chemistry books.

It was Tom's dream at the very young age of twelve to become a telegrapher, able to send messages across the country using Morse Code, a series of sounds reproduced over electrical wires. At the age of sixteen, his dream came true when he was hired as a telegraph operator by the Grand Trunk Railway.

While he learned to telegraph faster than anyone else in the business, he kept up with his scientific studies. In 1869 Tom patented his first inventions, a vote recorder and stock exchange ticker, both of which were seen as advances in technology and engineering.

Tom, however, was more than just a scientist. He was also a businessman. Not only did he invent the new stock ticker, for instance, he also set up a company that could manufacture and sell it. Pope, Edison & Company, which was located in Menlo Park, New Jersey, was one of the first firms of electrical engineers in the country. In this way, Tom helped to carry out an important transition in nineteenth-century science, away from the solitary life of inventing to that of working with specialized research teams.

From his laboratory in Menlo Park and later in West Orange, Tom combined his passion for knowledge with a practical, down-to-earth nature. "Genius is one percent inspiration and ninety-nine percent perspiration" was his motto, and he lived by those words, spending endless hours to get an invention right, no matter what the cost. Tom's first wife, Mary Stilwell, whom he married in 1871, spent many nights alone while her husband slaved over every new inspiration.

95

There were many ground-breaking inventions that came out of Tom's laboratory. He devised a carbon telephone transmitter, which reproduced the sound of a human voice with incredible clarity. He vastly improved the carbon filament light bulb and invented a new system of electrical distribution—both of which were key developments in the modern electronics revolution. The phonograph, an improved storage battery, a dictating machine, and a mimeograph machine all came out of the Edison laboratories.

Tom spent much of the last years of his life attempting to protect the patents on his many inventions. He was involved in many lawsuits with various companies, including Bell Telephone and General Electric. When he died, of gastric ulcers, he was eighty-four. In 1960 he was elected to the Hall of Fame at New York University.

WILLIAM FAULKNER

NOVELIST

BORN *New Albany, Mississippi, September 25, 1897*

DIED *Oxford, Mississippi, July 6, 1962*

"It is [the writer's] privilege to help man endure by lifting his heart, by reminding him of the courage and honor and hope and pride and compassion and pity and sacrifice which have been the glory of his past." Those words, spoken by William Faulkner as he accepted the 1949 Nobel Prize for Literature, are characteristic of an author who wrote about a part of America's past with a unique passion and vision.

William was born and raised in the American South at one of the most unsettling junctures in its history. After the bitter, bloody Civil War and the difficult Reconstruction period, the South, as a community, was no longer a united society. Its fabric, which was based on slavery and the wealth of plantation owners, had been destroyed. The people of the South, both black and white, were now struggling to come to grips with their new positions. Some were poor who had been rich; some had power who had once been brutalized.

William himself would carry that conflict with him throughout his life. His own personal confusion stemmed from the fact that although he abhorred slavery, he was still deeply loyal to his homeland and his people. Such feelings would express themselves in the moral struggles of his characters and the world he created for them.

Unlike many of his contemporaries, Ernest Hemingway and F. Scott Fitzgerald among them, William lived an isolated, introspective life. He spent almost his entire life in the small town of Oxford, Mississippi, just forty miles from the town in which he was born.

William had never enjoyed school as a boy. In fact, by the time he was in eighth grade, he was absent more often than in class. He nearly graduated from high school, but dropped out after his second attempt at the eleventh grade. He developed his gift for writing by reading books by as many different authors as he could manage.

But more than education, it was William's own imagination that gave him the power to write. Feeling lost in his own community, he was driven to invent a whole life within his work. He created an entire community—Yoknapatawpha County, Mississippi—which he would explore in thirteen novels and dozens of stories.

Yoknapatawpha, population 15,611 and scattered over 2,400 miles, was William's metaphor for the moral struggles of his ancestors and neighbors. In addition, he described the universal, eternal human emotions of self-doubt, greed, and passion through the characters who lived within this mythical kingdom in northern Mississippi.

This community of people was vividly described in the lush, metaphor-rich prose that was Faulkner's hallmark. Some of his best-loved works include *Absalom, Absalom!*, *As I Lay Dying*, and *The Sound and the Fury*, each of which explores the social and moral conflicts of the people of Yoknapatawpha County from a different perspective.

Although he was eventually the winner of two Pulitzer Prizes, his work as a novelist was not very profitable, especially during the early part of his career. With a wife and children to support, as well as his extended family of three brothers whom he occasionally helped financially, William was always in need of money.

Like many other writers of this era, he went to Hollywood to work for the burgeoning new movie industry. He wrote many screenplays over the years, including adaptations of the works of Hemingway *(To Have and Have Not)*, Raymond Chandler *(The Big Sleep)*, and others.

Despite William's deeply personal inner conflicts, he was known to be a kind and generous man, both to his family and friends. Yet he also drank quite heavily. In and out of sanitoriums, he spent his life between bouts of alcoholism and great moments of genius. When he died at the age of sixty-four, he left behind a body of work—twenty-six books and many stories—that stands as a testament to a grand imagination and a unique American voice.

HENRY FORD

INDUSTRIALIST, AUTOMOBILE MANUFACTURER

BORN *Dearborn, Michigan, July 30, 1863*

DIED *Dearborn, Michigan, April 7, 1947*

"I invented the modern age," Henry Ford once said, and in many ways, he did just that. By mass-producing the Model T automobile, he altered the fabric of American life forever. Before Henry Ford's inventions, only the rich could afford to drive in "horseless carriages." But because he could produce the Model T inexpensively, over fifteen million Americans purchased one within twenty years.

The inventor of this modern-age miracle was the son of an Irish immigrant, William Ford, and his wife, Mary Litogot. Wil-

Henry Ford (left) and Harvey Firestone

liam and Mary settled in a small town outside Detroit, Michigan, where William ran a farm. He hoped that his son, Henry, born in 1863, would also become a farmer.

Henry, however, had no love for the land. Instead, he was forever tinkering with all things mechanical. According to some sources, Henry's father gave him a watch for his twelfth birthday. Within days, Henry had taken it apart and put it back together. Exactly how things were made, and how he might improve them, intrigued Henry throughout his life.

Henry attended a one-room schoolhouse in Dearborn. When he was sixteen, and felt he'd had enough of schooling and farm life, he walked six miles to the bustling city of Detroit. There he learned various industrial trades—electrical engineering and machinery among them—while working on his own inventions in his spare time. The newly invented gasoline-driven engine fascinated him, and he struggled to improve it. He attended a business school, for some financial background that might later be useful in his career, before returning to Dearborn to help his father run the farm.

Within a few years, however, Henry finally finished building his first locomotives and moved back to Detroit. He and two other inventors were building racing cars, and Henry began attracting attention for his exploits on the track. But Henry's real dream had always been to manufacture a car that the average man could afford, and he founded the Ford Motor Company to do just that.

The process by which Henry built his famous cars was truly innovative. In fact, Henry was the first to use a moving assembly line, in which men were lined up along a conveyor belt, each working on a particular task as it came down the line. This method saved hundreds of hours of work—an entire automobile could be produced in just ninety-three minutes.

The success of the Model T made Henry Ford one of the richest men and Ford Motor Company one of the largest corporations in the United States. Despite his brilliance, however, Henry Ford also had a stubborn nature, one that often kept his company from moving ahead as quickly as it might have. For nearly twenty years, for instance, the Model T was the only car Ford produced, while other car companies were offering different styles and more powerful engines.

In fact, Henry Ford was a most contradictory and difficult man. He held complete power over all who worked for him and was given to firing, without prior notice, even his most trusted workers. While Ford Motor Company offered some of the highest wages in Detroit—five and six dollars per day—Henry resisted all attempts to unionize his plant during the 1930s. Another unfortunate aspect of his personality was a considerable streak of anti-Semitism that turned many of his admirers away in disgust.

Although some of his ideas about politics and social issues were not commendable, Henry Ford did indeed usher in the modern age with his inventions.

JOHN FORD

FILM DIRECTOR

BORN *Cape Elizabeth, Maine, February 1, 1895*

DIED *Palm Desert, California, August 31, 1973*

"I simply direct pictures, and if I had my way, every morning of my life I'd be behind that camera at nine o'clock waiting for the boys to roll 'em, because that's the only thing I really like to do." In a career that spanned sixty years, John Ford directed scores of feature films and documentaries, which earned seventy-two Academy Award nominations and won twenty-three, six of which went to Ford personally. He was responsible for creating not only the screen personas of several key stars, most prominently John Wayne and Henry Fonda, but an extraordinary num-

---

John Ford (center) with James Stewart and John Wayne on the set of The Man Who Shot Liberty Valance

ber of America's favorite and most enduring pictures, among them *The Informer, The Grapes of Wrath,* and the classic Westerns *Stagecoach* and *The Searchers.*

It was the Western—a uniquely American genre—that became John Ford's forté. The story of the American frontier, in all its color and excitement, filled John Ford's imagination and, in turn, his movie screen.

John Ford was born Sean Aloysius O'Feeney to Irish immigrant parents in Cape Elizabeth, Maine. He was the last of thirteen children and, like his parents, spoke both Gaelic and English. He changed his name to Jack when he was playing high school football because he thought it sounded "tougher" than Sean. And he adopted Ford as his surname when he followed his older brother out to Hollywood when unable to join the U.S. Naval Academy.

Hollywood's film industry was just beginning to grow when John got his first job as a property man at Universal City in 1914. He filled in as Indian, soldier, and horseback rider in a number of films. He carried props, tended the camera—and learned everything he could about filmmaking. By the end of the year, he had become an assistant director, then was assigned to direct short films and Westerns. Offered a contract with Fox, he began to direct feature films in 1919.

John's first major film, *The Iron Horse,* established him as a leading director. Themes that would recur in his later work—the spirit of the pioneers, a strong sense of family bonds, loyalty to a cause, and the virtues of courage and honor—appeared in this silent film about the American railroad. His true genius was his ability to create simple and striking characters whose true personalities were revealed under the strain of war or through love and friendship.

Despite the fame that grew with every picture, he lived an unpretentious, if somewhat rowdy, life. He was a hard-drinking

104

man and made friends who had equal reputations as carousers. John Wayne, Johnny Weismuller, and Ward Bond were three actors with whom he both drank and worked. He always dressed in shabby clothes, wearing well-worn sneakers and could always be seen smoking a pipe. He rarely raised his voice on the set, and worked with a friendly economy of words that revealed itself on the screen as clear and precise direction. Off the screen, he was a happily married man, wedded to the same woman, Mary McBryde Smith, from 1920 until he died in 1973.

John's contributions to American cinema cannot be overestimated. Many of the world's finest contemporary filmmakers look at his work as the pinnacle of moviemaking. Orson Welles, when asked which American directors most appealed to him, replied "the old masters. By which I mean John Ford, John Ford, John Ford." The French director François Truffaut, who died in 1984, summed up John's career this way, ". . . John Ford knew how to make the public laugh . . . or cry. The only thing he didn't know how to do was to bore them." John died of cancer on August 31, 1973, after a long and distinguished career.

BENJAMIN FRANKLIN

INVENTOR, STATESMAN, PHILOSOPHER

BORN *Boston, Massachusetts, January 17, 1706*

DIED *Philadelphia, Pennsylvania, April 17, 1790*

One of America's most versatile and respected founding fathers was Benjamin Franklin. With his ability as a foreign ambassador, domestic statesman, and scientist, he changed the course of our history.

Ben was the tenth son of Josiah Franklin, a candlemaker who moved from England to Boston around 1682 or 1683. Although the family had enough money to send Ben to school for a few years, the expense soon grew too great and, when he was ten, Ben was brought into the candlemaking business. Later, at the

---

Benjamin Franklin signing the Declaration of Independence

age of twelve, he was apprenticed to his brother James's printing shop.

He at once showed a remarkable talent and love for printing —and for the written word. When James started a small newspaper, Ben fashioned a thoughtful essay and slipped it anonymously under the door of the shop. Much to his delight, it was printed.

Once Ben had gained confidence in his own ability, he saved enough money to move to Philadelphia, the sophisticated center of the Colonies. He was only seventeen and had just a dollar and a copper shilling in his pocket.

It was here that Ben Franklin, a poor unknown Bostonian, rose to fame, wealth, and influence. Using the skills he had obtained in his brother's shop and money he had borrowed from friends, he eventually set himself up as an independent printer and publisher. His good humor and generous nature soon made him many friends, and won him the love of a young Philadelphian named Deborah Read, with whom he lived until her death in 1774.

Ben proved to be an adept businessman. His shop and newspaper made money, and his fame as an intellectual grew throughout Philadelphia and the rest of the country. His most famous publication, *Poor Richard's Almanack*, remains a perfect example of Ben's talents as a writer, philosopher, and observer of human nature. Chock full of catchy phrases like "Early to bed and early to rise, makes a man healthy, wealthy, and wise," the *Almanack* sold 10,000 copies a year and made Franklin's name a household word.

Although Ben never campaigned for public office, he was too public-spirited to avoid such commitments. He was appointed to a number of different offices, including clerk for the Pennsylvania Assembly and postmaster general for the Colonies.

His talent for problem solving extended to the scientific world as well. Seeing a need for a better heating system for Pennsylvania's cold winter homes, Ben invented the Franklin stove. He perhaps is best known for his early experiments with electricity. Ben's discovery that electricity was a "single fluid" and his invention of the first electric battery pushed research years ahead, and provided the groundwork for technology we take for granted in the twentieth century.

Ben would have been happy to continue with his endeavors in Philadelphia if the events of the day had not become so pressing. When hints of war between the Colonies and the English crown became serious threats, Ben was sent to England to negotiate. He spent nine years attempting to settle the disputes, but the seeds of unrest had already been planted and the English resisted a peaceful solution. After his wife died in 1774, Ben returned to the Colonies and stayed to help his country during the Revolution.

Named a member of the Second Continental Congress, Ben raised money for the army, then was sent abroad again—this time to France to seek its support for the Revolutionary cause. Ben's renown preceded him to France, and his mere presence intensified popular enthusiasm for the cause. He was able not only to gain support for the revolution, but to secure desperately needed loans to help the new country grow. He returned a hero in 1785.

In the final years of his life, Ben continued to guide his country toward liberty and good government. He was a member of the Constitutional Convention, chosen to help frame the new system of democracy in the United States. Since compromise needed to prevail over hot tempers and passions, his immense prestige and formidable skills as a diplomat were of great value. He died at the age of eighty-four.

BUCKMINSTER FULLER

INVENTOR

B O R N *Milton, Massachusetts, July 12, 1895*
D I E D *Los Angeles, California, July 1, 1983*

"Man can do anything he needs to do . . . man can create miracles." No one was ever truer to these words than the man who wrote them, Buckminster Fuller. He invented cars, houses, and maps while becoming one of America's most original philosophers.

Buckminster was born into a distinguished, wealthy New England family. Handicapped by poor vision, Buckminster was fitted for his first pair of eyeglasses at the age of four, allowing him to see clearly for the first time. He would later recall, "I was filled with wonder at the beauty of the world and I have never lost my delight in it."

In school he was best in math and science. By the time he was in kindergarten, he was already building things out of tetrahedral blocks—blocks with four sides, shaped like pyramids. They would later be a key to his most famous invention—the geodesic dome.

Buckminster never did get a college degree. He was kicked out of Harvard University twice—once for poor grades and once for going to New York and spending all his tuition money on a lavish party for the cast of the Ziegfeld Follies show. After serving in the Navy, he began his lifelong marriage to Anne Hewlett and went to work for her father, an architect and manufacturer.

When Buckminster's four-year-old daughter died in 1922, he began to drink heavily. He was unemployed, penniless, and on the verge of suicide. But then he told himself, "You do not have the right to eliminate yourself. You belong to the universe."

He turned his energies instead to studying the basic design principles of nature—physics and other natural sciences—intending to use his knowledge to help mankind. He stopped drinking, slept only two hours a night, and spoke to no one—not even his wife—for nearly two years. He was trying to find new ways of thinking and of expressing himself.

What Buckminster concluded was that the essence of all things is in how they are designed. Iron, for instance, is iron and not another metal because of the way its atoms are arranged. As people develop ways of better arranging atomic patterns, he reasoned, they could do "more with less and less."

Buckminster began to invent things that could make life easier and less expensive for the average person. His "Dymaxion House" could be easily moved and mass-produced, and featured glass outer walls, automatic vacuum cleaners, and a shower that recycled its own water. His "Dymaxion Car" had three wheels, could go 120 miles per hour, and was one of the safest, most easily steered cars ever made. While these inventions never became popular, he earned professional respect from other scientists.

But it was his geodesic dome that made Buckminster both rich and famous. Basically a circle or sphere, the dome is made up of many tetrahedrons resembling his old kindergarten building blocks. Combining the two shapes, he invented a form that was incredibly strong without being incredibly heavy. Used to create buildings of any type, this form can be built to any size, and will withstand both desert heat and Arctic cold.

The dome made Buckminster Fuller an internationally famous figure. He lectured all over the world about man's relationship to technology and the importance of conserving our natural resources. He considered both population control and the energy crisis to be problems of "ignorance," and said that with the right technology, the whole world could live happily in the area the size of the small island nation of Haiti.

Until the end of his life, Buckminster Fuller was an inspiring example of what the liberated human mind and spirit could do. In 1983, while visiting his wife of over sixty years in the hospital, he suffered a fatal heart attack. Anne passed away two days later.

111

CLARK GABLE

ACTOR

BORN *Cadiz, Ohio, February 1, 1901*

DIED *Hollywood, California, November 16, 1960*

The "King" of the movies in the 1930s and 1940s was indisputably Clark Gable, an actor with such strong masculinity and debonair manner that both hard-bitten "macho" men and starry-eyed females fell for him on sight. As Rhett Butler in *Gone With the Wind*, a lighthearted, romantic journalist in *It Happened One Night*, and a villainous cowboy in *The Painted Desert*, Clark brought his own special qualities to the screen.

William Clark Gable was born in Cadiz, Ohio, the only child of William Gable, an oil contractor, and Adeline Hershelman.

Clark was a shy and awkward boy, very studious and not particularly popular with his classmates. He kept to himself, rarely taking part in school activities or sports. Instead, he studied hard, concentrating on the sciences and planning a career in medicine.

During his freshman year at college, however, Clark met up with two members of a traveling theater company then playing in Akron. Their conversations about stage life sparked Clark's imagination and he began spending every waking minute at the theater. As he later told a reporter, "I forgot all my ideas about becoming a doctor when I made my first appearance on the stage."

Success didn't come easily for Clark; it took years of hard work before he got his big break. After an unsuccessful try on Broadway, he worked with the Jewell Players, a traveling theater company, for only fourteen dollars a week. Later, when that company went bankrupt, he hopped a freight train to Oregon and went from one odd job to another—earning money as a lumberjack, a timekeeper at a telephone company, and an errand boy in a newspaper office—while performing with the poor but earnest Portland theater company.

113

When he made his way back to Broadway a few years later, his luck changed and he attracted the attention of many critics. One review described him as "young, vigorous and brutally masculine" in one play, and in another his performance intrigued the renowned actor Lionel Barrymore. Barrymore was so impressed with Clark that he arranged for him to have a screen test in Hollywood.

Clark, despite rather noticeably large ears, fit the needs of a burgeoning film industry. His deep, gravelly voice and good looks were perfect for the action pictures that began to pour out of Hollywood. Starring in eleven films in just three years, Clark went on to play opposite some of the most beautiful and famous leading ladies—Greta Garbo, Jean Harlow, and Claudette Colbert to name but a few.

Clark quickly became the heartthrob of the nation, with millions of women swooning over his roguish smile and twinkling blue eyes. But Clark had only one great love, the actress and film comedienne Carole Lombard, whom he married in 1939. The couple lived together happily until Carole was tragically killed in a plane crash just three years later.

One week after her death, Clark announced that he would leave show business to join the Army. After graduating from the Air Force's Officer Candidate School, he flew five bomber combat missions, for which he received the Distinguished Flying Cross and the Air Medal.

When Clark returned to Hollywood, he was ready to resume his career with enthusiasm and vigor. He went on to make some of America's best-loved films, including *Teacher's Pet* with Doris Day and *The Misfits* with Marilyn Monroe.

Known for his down-to-earth good humor and professional integrity, he was also modest, never forgetting his early days as a struggling actor before becoming a star. Even after he became famous, he always adorned his dressing room with mementos of earlier days as a struggling actor. Across them, he wrote: "Just to remind you, Gable." Luckily for us, he has left over sixty films to remember him by.

114

JOHN KENNETH GALBRAITH

ECONOMIST, AUTHOR

B O R N *Near Iona Station, Ontario, Canada, October 15, 1908*

Known as a distinguished professor of economics, John Kenneth Galbraith has had influence far beyond the classroom, forever changing the way Americans look at the relationship between economics and democracy. Moreover, his clear, witty writing and speaking styles have made the study of economics more accessible to generations of Americans.

John was born on a small farm in Ontario, Canada, the only son of William and Catherine Galbraith. He has fond memories of his youth, spent doing chores on the farm and joining his parents at the Baptist church every Sunday. Athletic and agile, even at the towering height of six-eight, John has remained an avid swimmer and skier.

In fact, he was so enamored with farm life that when he graduated from his tiny local high school, he majored in animal husbandry (the study of animal breeding and raising) at the Ontario Agricultural College. He later transferred to the University of Toronto, from which he graduated with a bachelor of science degree in 1931.

With degree in hand at the age of twenty-three, John moved to the United States to study at the University of California at Berkeley. It was here that his love affair with U.S. political affairs and education began, and he soon applied for and received his American citizenship. He received a master's degree and a Ph.D. in agricultural economics, then began his professional career as an instructor and tutor at Harvard and Princeton universities.

Teaching for John became intertwined with government service and authorship of many texts, essays and novels. In the 1940s, he worked for the U.S. Government in a variety of posts, among them economic adviser to the National Defense Advisory Committee and deputy administrator in the Office of Price Administration.

Rejoining the faculty of Harvard University in 1949, where he would remain throughout most of his career, John's own economic theories became the focus of a number of books and essays. In particular, he would publish three works that would affect the course of American economic activity and political activity in the 1960s and early 1970s.

American Capitalism: The Concept of Countervailing Power, *The Affluent Society,* and *The New Industrial State* outlined his theories about the link between the free-market system of capitalism practiced in America and the effect it has on the way we live. John believes that without the intervention of such opposing groups as labor unions and government controls, corporations would have nothing to stop them from increasing their prices on a continuing basis, raising the cost of living uncontrollably.

John's theories also focused on how America, one of the wealthiest nations in the world, was squandering its resources on largely unnecessary consumer goods and ignoring more fundamental needs, like clean air and water, decent housing, and adequate support for the arts and sciences. He called for using more of America's wealth for such public-sector needs, and many of his suggestions and theories were highlighted during the Great Society administration of President Lyndon Johnson.

In addition to his work as an educator, John took an active part in politics. President John Kennedy appointed him as ambassador to India in 1961, where he served for two years. Once referring to himself as an "independent operator at the guerrilla level of American politics," John also supported many liberal candidates, including Adlai Stevenson, John Kennedy, and Eugene McCarthy, and causes such as ending the war in Vietnam, civil rights, women's issues and environmental protection.

Although his theories have come under attack by many conservative economists, John's work as an economist and concerned American citizen remains influential. Now retired from professional life, he lives in Cambridge, Massachusetts.

G E O R G E
G E R S H W I N

C O M P O S E R

B O R N *New York, New York, September 26, 1898*

D I E D *Beverly Hills, California, July 11, 1937*

One of the first modern composers to fuse American black jazz and spiritual traditions with classical and popular music, George Gershwin created wholly original American musical forms. Broadway, Hollywood, and the classical music world have all been enriched by his contributions.

Born in New York City of Russian immigrant parents, George was the second son of four children. He was not a particularly musical youngster, preferring to spend time playing street hockey and basketball with friends and enjoying the hustle and bustle of an active city.

George (left) and Ira Gershwin

When George was twelve, his family bought a piano for his older brother, Ira, who had expressed an interest in learning the instrument. George immediately showed great promise as a musician. It was the gifted music teacher Charles Hambitzer who first recognized both George's young talent and his driving desire to learn. Hambitzer wrote in a letter to his sister, "I have a new pupil who will make his mark in music if anybody will. The boy is a genius, without a doubt. He's just crazy about music and can't wait until it's time to take his lesson." George's perseverance paid off at a young age—by the time he was fourteen, he was playing piano professionally in a resort in the Catskill Mountains.

In 1914, George became the youngest staff pianist at Remick, a music publishing house in the heart of New York's music publishing world, nicknamed Tin Pan Alley. At the princely sum of fifteen dollars a week, he worked with countless songwriters who turned out tune after popular tune for Remick.

The following year, George left the company to start his own career as a composer. Joining the publishing house of Harms, George was paid $35 a week to write as many songs as he was able. Here, George composed his first big hit, "Swanee," and by the time he went off on his own in the early 1920s, he was ready to take on the world.

With his brother Ira and other lyricists, George composed some of the most memorable music of that era: "I'll Build a Stairway to Paradise," "I've Got a Crush on You," " 'S Wonderful," and many other popular hits used on Broadway and in Hollywood films. Together, the Gershwin brothers also wrote the music and lyrics for *Of Thee I Sing*, the first musical ever to receive a Pulitzer Prize.

In the midst of their most popular successes, George decided to attempt the classical work he had always yearned to create. By 1924, he had written *Rhapsody in Blue*, a classical jazz piece that has become universally regarded as a truly original piece of mu-

119

sic. Another of his successes was *An American in Paris,* later made into an Academy Award-winning film of the same name.

Although the list of Gershwin hits is almost endless, the opera *Porgy and Bess* perhaps most endures. Telling a moving story of a struggling family of rural Southern blacks, George and Ira used American speech and jazz rhythms to create a distinctly American opera. In addition to his collaboration with Ira, George frequently worked with Dubose Heyward, who also received credit for "Summertime," one of *Porgy and Bess*'s most moving songs.

Working with incredible intensity, George's energy was unflagging. In 1937, while working on yet another movie musical, he began to suffer painful headaches. After exploratory surgery in which an inoperable brain tumor was found, he died at the age of thirty-eight. As one epitaph read, "Gershwin may have died leaving many a masterwork unwritten, but not before he had achieved his destiny."

SAMUEL GOLDWYN

MOTION PICTURE PRODUCER

B O R N *Warsaw, Poland, August 27, 1882*

D I E D *Los Angeles, California, January 31, 1974*

Samuel Goldwyn was born into a poor family in Warsaw, Poland. Orphaned at a young age and left to fend for himself, he ran away, first to London and then to America. This ambitious Polish immigrant would become one of the greatest motion picture producers in Hollywood history—a true pioneer in a new American industry.

At the age of thirteen, Sam, newly arrived in the United States, got a job in a glove factory in upstate New York. Learning English at night and the manufacturing business during the day,

Sam had become a U.S. citizen and was widely considered one of the best glove salesmen in the world by the time he was twenty.

Sam could have written his own ticket in the glove business had he stayed with it. Instead, he chose another career altogether —the movies. He formed a partnership with his wife Blanche's brother, Jesse Lasky, a vaudeville producer. Together they entered one of the fastest-growing industries in America: motion picture production.

With $26,000 as capital, Jesse and Sam formed the Jesse Lasky Feature Play Company. At that time, 1912–14, they had very little competition—filmmaking was still in the experimental stages and had not caught on with either the public or business community. In fact, their film, *The Squaw Man,* was the very first full-length feature film produced in the United States. In the next few years, movies would become a multimillion dollar business.

After making a number of successful films with Lasky, Sam sold his share of the corporation for a reported $900,000. With this profit, Sam began a new company, Goldwyn Pictures Corporation in 1918. Two years later, with the assistance of other investors, he left to found Eminent Authors Pictures, Inc., a new film company which put its emphasis on the importance of good screenwriting, a trademark of Sam's filmmaking philosophy.

In 1925 he formed yet another company, Metro-Goldwyn-Mayer, with Louis B. Mayer. Some of America's best-loved movie musicals were made in this studio, but Sam left the company only a year later to form Samuel Goldwyn Presents, a company in which he finally had total control.

Because of Sam's respect for writers, he attracted some of the best-known writers of the day to Hollywood. Sam also had a knack for discovering great talent on the screen and behind the camera as well. Gary Cooper, Tallulah Bankhead, and Rudolph Valentino were just a few of the stars he showcased. John Ford,

Howard Hawks, and William Wyler, some of the best film directors in history, also made many of their films with Sam Goldwyn.

Sam now began to make the films for which he would go
down in history—*All Quiet on the Western Front, The Little Foxes,
Pride of the Yankees,* and *The Best Years of Our Lives,* which won
an Oscar for best picture in 1946, among many others. The Goldwyn studio became a symbol of excellence in the industry, largely
due to Sam's insistence on using only the best directors, writers,
and technicians for each of his films.

In addition to being a dynamic and innovative producer,
Sam had a rather sharp wit and temperamental behavior on the
movie set. He was also known for a clever misuse of words that
bordered on the hilarious. Labeled "Goldwynisms," these phrases
soon became Hollywood lore. "Include me out!" has been attributed to Sam, as has the famous Goldwyn dictums, "In two words,
im possible!" and "I'll give you a definite maybe." He died in
1974, three years after being awarded the Presidential Medal of
Freedom.

123

BERRY GORDY, JR.

RECORD PRODUCER

BORN *Detroit, Michigan, November 28, 1929*

Perhaps no other recording company the world has had as much influence on the American rock and roll industry as Motown Records, created by a very determined young man named Berry Gordy, Jr. Diana Ross, Michael Jackson, and Lionel Richie are just a few of the artists who have passed through the doors of Motown under Berry's creative influence.

Berry Gordy grew up in a poor black ghetto in Detroit, where opportunities for young black men were scarce. Berry was lucky in at least two respects: He was equipped with a sharp

Berry Gordy (right) and performer Smokey Robinson

intelligence and drive, and he had a large and loving family who supported his goals.

Berry never finished high school, dropping out in his junior year to become a featherweight boxer. He was drafted into the Army in 1951, and during his service, Berry not only earned his high school diploma, but also developed a fine ear for great jazz music. When he was discharged, he returned to Detroit and opened a record store that featured jazz recordings.

It wasn't long, however, before the store went bankrupt, and Berry took a job as a plasterer with his father. He realized that his business failed because jazz was not particularly popular in the late 1950s. Instead, Elvis Presley, Bill Haley and the Comets, and other rock and rollers were hot. However, many of them used rhythms and vocal techniques that could be traced to black musical forms.

Berry knew that equally talented singers and songwriters were largely unknown because they were black—because of racism, black performers were never given recording contracts with major, white-owned companies. At the same time, he felt that the black sound would have a large audience if given the chance. Listening carefully to popular music, he began to write his own songs, including many that became big hits, like "Lonely Teardrops" and "You Got What it Takes."

A young singer, William "Smokey" Robinson, Jr., first gave Berry the idea of producing his own records, an occupation practically unheard of for a black man at that time. Borrowing $700 from his family, Berry put up a sign that read "Hitsville USA," founding Motown (a play on "Motor Town," a nickname for Detroit) Records in 1959.

Though he had no formal business training, Berry did have a keen eye for talent, and an instinct for what would sell. He also had a strong will to succeed, which attracted other energetic black artists. Berry himself once described the music scene in Detroit as "rats, roaches, love, guts and talent . . . Motown is not just climbing out of poverty, escaping it— It's being young, creative, doing things with dignity. It's pride."

Under Berry's careful direction, a whole new sound emerged from his studios onto the American popular music scene. Rhythm and blues, gospel music, and rock and roll merged into a distinctive style during the 1960s: the Motown Sound. Berry took young black artists like Diana Ross and the Supremes and the Jackson 5, and helped make them into superstars. "Hitsville USA" became Motown Industries, one of the most successful black enterprises in the United States.

Although many of Motown's original artists have since left for other record companies, Motown Industries still thrives. Now diversified into the motion picture business, Berry and his company are now headquartered in Los Angeles, California. *Lady Sings the Blues*, produced in 1972, is Motown's most successful film to date, having won five Academy Award nominations.

Berry himself remains a very private person, staying out of the public spotlight as much as possible. A family man with a multimillion-dollar corporation, he is somewhat modest about his accomplishments. He did, however, make this comment about this work, "I made $367 million in sixteen years. I must be doing something right!"

BILLY GRAHAM

EVANGELIST

B O R N *Charlotte, North Carolina, November 7, 1918*

In 1970, evangelist Billy Graham was second only to President Richard Nixon in the Gallup Poll's "Most Admired Men in America." His deep religious commitment, combined with his fiery speaking style, have attracted millions of followers to his church. One of the first ministers to use modern media as the channel through which to preach, Billy Graham remains today an influential spiritual leader.

Billy grew up on a farm in North Carolina, the son of William Franklin and Morrow Graham. He spent his childhood like many other rural children; he loved the outdoors and spent much of his time doing farm chores and playing baseball.

Although Billy was an indifferent student in most subjects, he adored history, reading many books independently in his spare time. The summer after he graduated from high school, he took a number of part-time jobs to save money for college.

It wasn't until his sixteenth year that Christianity took on a deep, personal meaning for Billy. It was during a revival meeting conducted in Charlotte by a traveling preacher that Billy made his decision to devote his life to the fundamentalist church. Fundamentalists believe in a strict interpretation of the Bible and doctrines of the Christian faith.

After graduating from high school, he briefly attended the fundamentalist Christian Bob Jones University, but transferred to the Florida Bible Institute after one semester. In 1939, he was baptized a Baptist, then took to preaching around the Florida campus. A year later, he was officially ordained a minister.

His true career began after he received a degree in anthropology from the prestigious Wheaton College. Starting with a local radio show called "Songs in the Night," Billy began to build the media ministry that would bring him the attention of millions of Americans and the respect of many world leaders. The show was broadcast from 1944 to 1945 over a Chicago station.

Billy also began a series of "citywide campaigns"—personal appearances and rallies throughout the nation, to raise money for his own organization, the Billy Graham Evangelistic Association, from which he was paid a very modest salary.

Suddenly he was famous. Although some nonfundamentalist Christians were wary of his style, he won their respect by his honesty. He would only crusade in a particular city or town if the local pastor had invited him and, most important, he stressed the importance of going to local churches as a kind of follow-up to discovering Christ through Billy himself.

During the 1950s he hosted another radio program, published a series of inspirational and religious books, and wrote a daily personal advice column. His striking presence on television brought him even more followers and admirers.

In the 1960s Billy was drawn into the political debate over the burning issues of the day—segregation, the war in Vietnam, women's rights—here and around the world. His interpretation of these events and conditions were cast in light of his religious beliefs and biblical prophecies and comforted thousands of Americans during a troubled time.

It also brought him to the attention of American Presidents. His first invitation to the White House came from President Truman, and he has been invited back by nearly every President since. Billy enjoyed a special friendship with President Nixon and delivered a prayer at his inauguration in 1969.

In 1987 many fundamentalist churches were rocked by scandal. While the reputations of such popular preachers as Jim Bakker and Oral Roberts have been damaged, Billy Graham's integrity has remained unquestioned.

KATHERINE MEYER GRAHAM

NEWSPAPER PUBLISHER

BORN *New York, New York, June 16, 1917*

President of the Washington Post Company since 1963, Katherine Graham is one of America's most powerful women. Under her administration are two of the world's most influential media, the *Washington Post* and *Newsweek* as well as their parent corporation, the Washington Post Company.

It is doubtful that anyone would have predicted such an illustrious career for Kay. As a child growing up in Washington, she suffered from tuberculosis and spent much of her teenage years in bed, reading. A shy girl, Kay was overshadowed by her accomplished, domineering mother, Agnes Meyer, an author and philanthropist, and her father, Eugene Meyer, a banker with an equally strong personality.

Although Kay and her four siblings grew up in privileged circumstances, their parents' emphasis on civic responsibility was firmly ingrained. As Kay once told a reporter, "There was a great deal of emphasis . . . on having to *do* something. It never occurred to me that I didn't have to work."

After attending a private high school in Virginia, Kay entered Vassar College, then transferred to the University of Chicago. Working on student newspapers, Kay discovered a love for journalism and a passion for current events.

America was in the midst of one of its darkest eras, the Great Depression, when Eugene Meyer bought the *Washington Post* for $825,000 at an auction in 1933. Kay spent her summers during college working there until she graduated and took a job as a reporter for the *San Francisco News*. A year later she returned to Washington to join the editorial staff of the *Post*.

In 1940 Kay met and married lawyer Philip Graham. Although she kept a hand in at the *Post* while she was married, her career became less important than her husband and four children. In 1945 Eugene offered his son-in-law the job of associate publisher at the newspaper. Six months later Philip was made publisher, and in 1948 Eugene sold all his voting stock to his daughter and her husband.

Under Philip's administration, the *Post* continued to pursue the highest of journalistic standards. In addition, the newspaper and its related corporation, the Washington Post Company, were run at a profit. By 1961 it could afford to pay nearly $8,000,000 for *Newsweek* magazine.

By all accounts, Philip had an obsessive desire for success—again, Kay was nearly overshadowed by her husband's powerful personality. But perhaps Philip's ambition was more than he was

131

able to handle; after suffering from psychiatric problems, he committed suicide in 1963, leaving his wife in control of the Washington Post Company and all its holdings.

Despite her shyness and relative inexperience, Kay assumed the presidency of the company and, most importantly, of the *Washington Post* itself. The early years were especially tough for Kay. The newspaper business had always been run by men, and she was one of the first women to assume such a high position. But Kay was determined to learn the business of running a newspaper, and within ten years, the *Post* was reporting profits of more than $10 million. It had also attained a reputation as one of the finest newspapers in the world, rivaling the *New York Times.* It led the nation in covering some of the century's most controversial events, including the Pentagon Papers in 1971 and the Watergate scandal in 1972–74.

Today, in her seventies, Kay remains active, both professionally and socially. She keeps a close eye on the Post, and is known to throw some of Washington's most sophisticated parties. Despite her accomplishments, Kay remains modest. "Have I mastered my job?" she asked a reporter. "No one ever masters a job. I try to do the best I can. You just keep plugging away."

132

MARTHA GRAHAM

DANCER, CHOREOGRAPHER

BORN *Pittsburgh, Pennsylvania, May 1894*

"If a student comes to me and asks, 'Should I be a dancer?' I tell her, 'If you have to ask, you should not.' " From the time she was a tiny child, Martha Graham knew in her heart that she was meant to dance. At the age of two, according to some sources, Martha danced down the aisle at church services in Pittsburgh, where she lived until she was eight. Now in her nineties, Martha has been the most prominent figure in modern dance, bringing this art form to the forefront of American culture.

"Martha's sole purpose in her art is to awaken the awareness

Martha Graham (center), performing in "Deaths and Entrances" in 1944

of life," said one dance critic, "and for this end she has no formula and no set vocabulary of movements." Indeed, Martha's style of dance is like no other. She was trained by two of the most innovative dancers of the century, Ruth St. Denis and Ted Shawn. Their company, Denishawn, broke away from the forms of classical ballet and explored abstract movements set to contemporary music. Although just eight years old when she first saw them perform, Martha felt at once that she had found a home for her young talent. By the time she was in her early teens, she managed to convince her skeptical parents to enroll her in the Denishawn school in Los Angeles.

There she learned the discipline of her art, the intense physical training required for her body to perform the rigors of dance. Rehearsing six to eight hours a day, Martha developed the movements that would make her famous and create a whole new school of modern dance. Precise, standardized ballet steps were unnecessary to create the dances Martha imagined. Instead, a dancer's own deeply personal emotions were expressed in freer, more dramatic movements.

134 Martha's dances have attracted international acclaim since she first performed with Ted Shawn in 1920. After staying with Denishawn for a number of years, she broke away to perform in New York City with the Greenwich Village Follies. From there, her drive to create new dance forms led her to explore New Mexican Native American dances, the themes in the poetry of Emily Dickinson, and the scenic beauty in the paintings of Georgia O'Keeffe, among other diverse creative sources. From each of them Martha found inspiration and ideas for movements and themes for new dances.

Martha has choreographed nearly one hundred and fifty dances, some in collaboration with famous designers like the sculptor Isamu Noguchi, composers like Aaron Copland, and other dancers like George Balanchine. *Letter to the World, Appala-*

chian Spring, and *Frontier* are just a few of the most famous Graham inventions. Each has a different theme, but all include the marks of a Martha Graham dance—stark, angular movements made against a sparsely decorated set.

In addition to performing and creating dances, Martha has spent much of her life teaching others her craft. For almost sixty years, the Martha Graham Center of Contemporary Dance has trained modern dancers and influenced all aspects of contemporary dance, from classical ballet to the Broadway stage.

Although in her nineties, Martha Graham shows no signs of retiring. Her company performed two new Graham dances in 1986, when Martha celebrated the sixtieth anniversary of her stage debut.

ALEXANDER HAMILTON

POLITICAL LEADER

BORN *British West Indies, January 11, 1753–57 (disputed)*

DIED *Weehawken, New Jersey, July 12, 1804*

Honest, but arrogant, vain, but dedicated to public service, Alexander Hamilton helped lay the foundation for the American system of government that has endured for over two hundred years.

Alexander was a young man about twenty years old when he first came to America, leaving behind a painful childhood. He was born out of wedlock to Rachel Faucette, a West Indian, and a poor Scottish drifter named James Hamilton, who left the family when Alexander was just a boy. Rachel and her family were then treated as social outcasts, shunned by the community. The legacy of poverty and disgrace would forever haunt Alexander and lead him to mistrust others.

When Alexander arrived in America, he first enrolled in a prep school in New Jersey, then in King's College (now Columbia University) in New York City. He at once displayed a keen mind and remarkable writing ability. In fact, at the first hints of the Revolutionary War, Alexander set about writing some of the most important documents of the time, displaying great knowledge of history and politics.

As war with Britain became a certainty, Alexander joined the patriot cause with enthusiasm. He fought alongside George Washington and played a role in many important battles. Since his skills on the battlefield did not impress Washington as much as his talents with a pen, he was made an aide-de-camp, responsible for more administrative duties.

In this position, Alexander's flair for political theory and management skills were developed as he handled military organization. When the war was over, he would put his talents to work in helping to develop a system of government for the new United States of America.

Alexander was a Federalist, believing that a strong central government and a system of checks and balances within it were absolute necessities. His rather pessimistic view of mankind led him to believe that most men were ruled by greed and personal ambition. Men needed strong public institutions to channel their energies into public good. He was also a staunch defender of inherited personal wealth and property, leading many to think of him as an aristocrat who distrusted the "average" man.

When Alexander was appointed the first Secretary of the Treasury by President Washington, he was able to put many of his financial theories into effect. He helped set up the country's first stable monetary system and obtained the passage of a bill to establish the new nation's first national bank. Import taxes were levied on countries trading with the United States, and a tax was placed on whiskey and other domestic commodities. In these ways the United States was able to repay its war debts and begin to grow as a nation.

Alexander also had strong opinions about foreign policy. He believed that a large and strong army, preferably with himself at its head, was necessary to protect the United States from foreign attack. His interference in foreign policy and views on domestic affairs frequently angered Secretary of State Thomas Jefferson, and the two men had a long-standing personal and political feud.

Indeed, it was difficult for many people to like Alexander. Married into one of the most wealthy and influential New York families, he was seen by many as an arrogant snob. He had a sharp tongue, both on the political and personal subjects.

His attacks on one politician, in fact, actually led to his own death. Aaron Burr, a long-time opponent, finally tired of Alexander's persistent personal attacks and challenged him to a duel. Alexander's skill with a pistol failed him, and he was shot on July 11, 1804, and died on the following day—ending one of the most interesting political careers in American history.

ERNEST HEMINGWAY

WRITER

BORN *Oak Park, Illinois, July 21, 1899*

DIED *Ketchum, Idaho, July 2, 1961*

$\mathbf{F}$ew writers have so captured the American imagination as Ernest Hemingway. Perhaps the most influential writer of the twentieth century, he also led a colorful and highly publicized personal life.

Ernest was an idealistic, sensitive youth. He despised the hypocrisy he saw in his small hometown, and many of his later stories would center around the contrast between innocence and corruption.

After high school, Ernest tried to enlist in the Army during

World War I. Despite the fact that he was turned down because of a defective eye, Ernest made it to Europe anyway, as an ambulance driver for the American Red Cross in Italy.

Badly wounded at the front, Ernest fell in love with one of his nurses while recuperating. She broke the romance off, but about ten years later, their love affair was the subject of his most famous novel, *A Farewell to Arms.*

Ernest spent most of the 1920s in Europe as a newspaper correspondent. He led a romantic life in Paris, along with many leading writers, artists, and intellectuals of the time. Pablo Picasso, Ezra Pound, James Joyce, and Gertrude Stein are a few of the most famous Hemingway cohorts, some of whom became his close friends.

In Europe, Hemingway first perfected his terse, journalistic literary style. His sentences were short, his adjectives few and simple. His heroes were usually hard-hearted men who faced their failures honorably. Ernest's style perhaps worked best in the short story form. In Europe, he wrote one of his best early collections of stories, *In Our Time.* They featured the adventures of Nick Adams, a character based on Ernest himself.

In 1936 and 1937, Ernest became deeply involved in the Spanish Civil War. He raised money to buy ambulances for the anti-fascist forces and went to Spain, where he witnessed events that formed the background for one of his most dramatic novels. *For Whom the Bell Tolls* was written as a warning against fascism and a tragic rendering of what war had done to Spain. Ernest vividly depicted the massacres perpetrated by both sides in this story of an American volunteer for the Loyalists.

After working as a war correspondent in World War II, Ernest returned to his homes in Florida and Cuba to write *Across the River and into the Trees,* a bitter novel of war that critics and readers hated. His career as a writer seemed over.

Yet two years later, *The Old Man and the Sea* led to a Pulitzer Prize in 1953 and a year later, Ernest won the Nobel Prize for Literature. *The Old Man and the Sea,* written in classic Hemingway style, is a simple, heroic account of an old man's attempt to land a huge fish. It has become one of his most popular works.

In his final years, Ernest became increasingly depressed. Despite the fact that he could be a kind and generous man, he also had a cruel streak. He was known to be insulting to women and, throughout his life, alienated friends and colleagues with his fits of bad temper and despair. Drinking heavily, and deeply depressed, he committed suicide in 1961, leaving a legacy of innovative literary genius to intrigue and inspire generations.

KATHARINE HEPBURN

ACTRESS

BORN *Hartford, Connecticut, November 8, 1909*

The first lady of American cinema, Katharine Hepburn has been enchanting audiences on stage, in film, and on television for over sixty years. Born into a wealthy family in Connecticut, Kate has portrayed a fascinating array of women from every walk of life.

Her parents, Dr. Thomas Hepburn and Katharine Houghton Hepburn, were outspoken, dynamic individuals. Thomas, a pioneer in social hygiene, was a physician who focused on treating venereal diseases, and Katharine was a suffragist who fought for women's rights. Instilling in their children a sense of self-discipline and social responsibility, they treated Katharine and her four younger brothers and sisters in a no-nonsense manner and yet with much love and support.

Kate was educated at home by private tutors and at a private girls' academy in Hartford. Always a rebel and a tomboy, Kate was considered a minor troublemaker by many teachers. But she was a good student, able to enter the prestigious Bryn Mawr College, with her sights already set on the stage.

After graduating with a degree in dramatic arts in 1928, Kate toured in summer stock productions, honing her talent by studying with acting and dance instructors. She made her Broadway debut within a year, in an insignificant role in a play that ran for only two weeks. She worked steadily in other roles until Hollywood beckoned to her in 1932. Although the screen became her major vehicle, Kate continued to perform often on Broadway and in regional theaters with much success.

Signing a contract with RKO Pictures, Kate took the movie industry and audiences by storm. She received her first Oscar for the film *Morning Glory*, in which she played a stagestruck tomboy. It was only the third movie she had ever made. Within five years, Kate starred in over ten pictures, many of which have become American classics.

143

In 1937 Kate left RKO, mainly because executives there found her difficult to work with and did not appreciate her refusal of roles that didn't suit her. The self-assurance she portrayed on the screen was matched by her independent offstage personality, making her unique for a woman living in the 1930s.

The films she did decide to make are considered some of the best American comedy films in history, including *Holiday* and *The Philadelphia Story*. Later, she also took on challenging dramatic roles in such classics as *The African Queen, Suddenly Last*

Summer, and *The Lion in Winter,* for which she won an Oscar in 1968.

Kate has played queens and aristocrats, cowgirls and athletes, executives and lawyers. She has been paired with some of the most handsome and talented leading men in the business, including Cary Grant, Peter O'Toole, Humphrey Bogart, and Burt Lancaster. In 1975 she made a television movie with Laurence Olivier, *Love Among the Ruins,* considered one of the finest actors of our century, for which she won an Emmy.

It is, perhaps, her collaborations with Spencer Tracy that most endure. Tracy's roughhewn looks and earthy manner made him the perfect foil for Kate's more classic beauty and aristocratic aura. Together they made nine films, both comedies and dramas, one of which—*Guess Who's Coming to Dinner?*—won Kate her second Oscar.

Tracy and Hepburn were also paired offscreen as well. Throughout a long and difficult love affair, Kate stood by Tracy as he fought a losing battle with alcoholism, until he died in 1967.

Now in her late seventies, Kate remains active. She plays golf and tennis, is an avid bicyclist, and does not appear to think about retirement. In 1982 she won her fourth Oscar for her role in the movie *On Golden Pond.* One of her most recent projects was a television movie called *Mrs. Delafield Wants to Marry.* The recipient of four Oscars and eleven Oscar nominations, Kate Hepburn remains America's leading lady.

OLIVER WENDELL HOLMES, JR.

JURIST

BORN *Boston, Massachusetts, March 8, 1841*

DIED *Washington, D.C., March 6, 1935*

At a time when our nation's system of laws, embodied in the Constitution, was facing increasing demands of an ever-changing society, few men played a more important role than Oliver Wendell Holmes. An intelligent and insightful man, he served as a symbol of rational thought to a whole generation of legal and political thinkers. His judgments and opinions continue to affect political and social affairs today.

Son of the great American poet Oliver Wendell Holmes, Sr., Oliver grew up in a lively, intellectual home in Boston. Oliver himself, however, was a rather indifferent student, undisciplined even at Harvard from which he graduated in 1861.

Coming into adulthood at the time of the Civil War, Oliver joined the Massachusetts militia. A brave and aggressive soldier, Oliver was wounded in action three times. Although he declared war "an organized bore," he was strongly affected by his own battlefront experiences. He became cynical, believing that only the strongest men could and should survive.

After the war, Oliver turned to the law as a career, receiving his degree from Harvard Law School in 1866. The following year, he passed the bar exam and began his distinguished career. Always fascinated with the structure and meaning of law, Oliver was able to translate his own thoughtful explorations into unique essays and books.

"The life of the law," he once wrote, "has not been logic; it has been experience." After examining the history of law, he found that, contrary to opinion, law was not based on consistent rules, but rather on changeable, practical solutions to particular problems. Cases were frequently won or lost depending on the skill of the lawyers that argued them and what was practical at the time.

146

This approach to the law garnered Oliver worldwide acclaim, but it did have a darker side. Implying that those who were strongest would survive and the weaker would fail, this theory neglected the spirit of equal protection under the law, an important component of our Constitution.

Oliver briefly taught at Harvard Law School and then was appointed to the Massachusetts Supreme Court, a post he held for nineteen years. While on the bench, he wrote opinions about approximately 1300 cases and drew the attention of President Theodore Roosevelt. When a vacancy was available on the United States Supreme Court, Roosevelt appointed Oliver to the post.

Called the "Great Dissenter," Oliver often found that his

narrow reading of the law separated him from the majority opinions of the Court. Whether dealing with cases of free speech or anti-trust litigation, Oliver concentrated only on whether the law was Constitutional or not. In one opinion he wrote, "The criterion of constitutionality is not whether we view the law to be for the public good." Oliver felt that it was not the Court's job to decide whether or not a law was good or bad for the people, but only whether it was allowed under the United States Constitution.

Known as judicial restraint, this strict approach led many to think of Oliver as unfeeling. In truth, however, he was a rather sociable, kindly man who in later years was often surrounded by younger lawyers who admired his precise but passionate belief in our Constitution.

Today, Oliver's theories about the role of the Supreme Court are especially relevant and continue to be debated. An impressive, eloquent jurist, Oliver is still remembered for his personal integrity and sense of public service.

147

H A R R Y
H O U D I N I

M A G I C I A N

B O R N *Budapest, Hungary, March 24, 1874*

D I E D *Detroit, Michigan, October 31, 1926*

Hands shackled behind his back, ankles locked in irons, and ten pairs of handcuffs locking the fetters together, Harry Houdini was put inside a small closet to see if he could escape from these chains. Ten minutes later he stepped out a free man, the handcuffs locked one inside the other but none binding him.

During his fascinating career as one of America's greatest escape artists and magicians, Houdini released himself from countless straitjackets, escaped from the world's most secure prisons, and performed death-defying stunts all over the world.

Harry Houdini, readying himself for another escape with the help of authorities

Harry's real name was Ehrich Weiss and he was born to a poor Jewish family in Hungary. Samuel Weiss, a rabbi, and his wife Cecilia took their family to America soon after Ehrich was born and made their home for a short time in Appleton, Wisconsin. An impractical teacher, Samuel found caring for his wife and eight children a tremendous burden. He turned in despair to his most energetic and industrious son, Ehrich, who was only twelve at the time.

Promising to help his family, Ehrich left home the very next morning, determined to make lots of money. He worked his way east to New York City, where he shined shoes, and did odd jobs and farm labor. In the city, where the family reunited, Rabbi Weiss opened a small Hebrew school and Ehrich continued working to help with family finances. It was when Theo, Ehrich's younger brother, showed him a magic trick, however, that Ehrich's true vocation was revealed to him.

He became fascinated by magic, researching it in books and practicing whenever he could. After changing his name to Harry Houdini (Harry after "Ehrie," his Hungarian nickname, and Houdini after France's most famous magician, Robert Houdin), he and Theo teamed up as the Brothers Houdini and set out to make it in show business.

It was the golden age of vaudeville in America. Before television, before movies, before radio, there was vaudeville—acrobats and magicians, song-and-dance acts, and humorous skits were produced on stages across America by thousands of energetic performers. The Brothers Houdini had a difficult start, and spent months performing in tiny clubs (called dime museums) and carnival sideshows, with little financial success or popularity.

It was when Bess Rahner came into his life, however, that Harry's career really took off. She was not only the love of his life, marrying him just a few weeks after they met, but she also replaced Theo in the act. While Theo went off to pursue a solo career, the newly married Houdinis developed a terrific new show. Bess's smaller, more agile body was much more suited to the escape tricks Harry created, and her moral support helped propel Harry to superstardom.

Harry became known throughout the world not only for his incredible skills as a magician and escape artist, but also for his integrity as a performer. His audience came first. He knew how to excite and enthrall a crowd. He knew what it took to keep them on the edge of their seats, once for nearly three hours, while he loosed himself from whatever complicated configuration of locks and chains he was put in.

He died on Halloween at the age of fifty-two, from acute appendicitis, after a performance in Detroit, Michigan. Despite his skepticism about seances, he and Bess had planned an experiment in the supernatural—the spouse who died first would attempt to contact the other through a medium. Although Bess tried repeatedly and waited endlessly, she never heard from her husband from the beyond. She died in 1943.

L A N G S T O N
H U G H E S

P O E T ,   A U T H O R

B O R N *Joplin, Missouri, February 1, 1902*
D I E D *New York, New York, May 22, 1967*

“**I** wrote about love, about the steel mills where my stepfather worked, the slums where we lived, and the brown girls from the South,” Langston Hughes once said. A prolific and instinctive writer, Hughes was one of the first black authors to gain a wide readership in America. He wrote poetry, novels, plays, and essays of social commentary and protest—a significant body of literature that speaks of the black experience in America.

In the small city of Lawrence, Kansas, Langston was raised by both his maternal grandmother and by a childless couple after his parents separated when he was a young boy. Attending schools in Kansas and Illinois, Langston was a lonely child, one who found excitement and companionship in books.

By the time he reached high school, he had discovered his own talents as a writer. After serving as editor of Cleveland Central High's yearbook, Langston considered writing professionally when his first poem, "The Negro Speaks of Rivers," was published the year after he graduated.

In 1921, after spending a year in Mexico, Langston decided to study literature at Columbia University in New York City. Although his academic life in New York lasted only a year, he fell in love with Harlem, the primarily black neighborhood in Upper Manhattan. He lived there for a year, concentrating solely on his writing career for the first time.

Wanting to see more of the world before returning to school, Langston traveled to Europe, working as a waiter and a bus boy whenever he needed to make money. When he returned to the United States, he stayed with his mother in Washington, D.C., and worked as a bus boy in a hotel. There he met world-renowned poet Vachel Lindsay, a white man who helped Langston get published in prestigious poetry journals and introduced him to other leading writers of the day. Langston had also received a scholarship to Lincoln University in Pennsylvania, and graduated with a B.A. in 1929.

During the 1920s, a remarkable resurgence of interest in black culture and history, known as the Harlem Renaissance, took place, and Langston was at the forefront of the movement. As he became more confident of his talent as a writer, he produced plays, novels, and essays as well as poetry. While championing the cause of civil rights, Langston did not express bitterness at white racism, but laced his prose with an irony and sadness at the ignorance involved.

For the rest of his life, Langston would write of black America in a unique and important way. Drawing upon black folk history, he incorporated the sights and sounds of Harlem and the American South into moving poems and stories. He also experimented with using an assortment of musical rhythms, including jazz and blues, in his work. The result was an impressive new literary style that has since influenced several generations of writers.

In addition to publishing, Langston lectured extensively, traveling throughout the world to give poetry readings and speeches. Known as the O. Henry of Harlem, Langston Hughes died at the age of sixty-five of postoperative complications after prostate surgery.

L E E
I A C O C C A

B U S I N E S S M A N

B O R N *Allentown, Pennsylvania, October 15, 1924*

Perhaps the biggest Cinderella story of the 1980s business world concerns Lido Anthony Iacocca and the Chrysler Corporation. Bringing the auto company back from the verge of bankruptcy is a tale that belongs more to the industrial heyday of the 1800s than twentieth-century corporate America.

Lee is the son of Italian immigrants, who passed along to him their belief that America is a land of opportunity. Lee particularly looked up to his father, Nicola, a businessman who tried his hand at many different jobs. Working as a shoemaker, running

a hot dog restaurant, and making a fortune as a real estate inves-
tor, Nicola finally lost his money in the Great Depression of the
1930s.

Nicola's ambition—and his abiding interest in automobiles
—rubbed off on his son. As a child, Lee enjoyed sports most of
all, but rheumatic fever at age fifteen left him with a heart condition and forced him to give up athletics forever.

Instead, Lee concentrated on his studies and became a champion debater. His bout with rheumatic fever kept him out of
World War II, but he studied all the harder, and earned engineering degrees from Lehigh and Princeton universities.

Lee then went to work for the Ford Motor Company as an
engineer, then switched to its sales department in Pennsylvania.
He worked hard, and by the time he was thirty-six had earned the
title of vice president and general manager.

Lee's crowning achievement of his career at Ford was his
development of the Mustang. This affordable sports car was introduced in 1964 and quickly became one of the bestselling cars
ever. In 1970 Lee Iacocca was named president of Ford, second
in command only to Chairman Henry Ford II himself.   155

But Ford, like the rest of the American car industry, was hit
hard when the price of oil was driven up by the organization of
Middle Eastern oil exporters (OPEC). More damaging to Lee was
a feud between him and his powerful boss, Henry Ford II. He was
fired in 1978, after a long fight which left both men bitter.

Like his father, Lee landed on his feet. Before the year was
out, he was running the Chrysler Corporation. Many people considered it a dubious honor, as Chrysler was the smallest of the Big
Three car companies. It was also the slowest to adjust to the new
era of smaller, more fuel-efficient cars. With the second great gas
shortage in 1979, the company nearly went under. In 1980 alone,
it lost $1.7 billion dollars.

Lee immediately cut operating costs by laying off workers

and adopting various cost-cutting measures, but the company re-mained in grave danger. To fund a line of new economy cars, Lee appealed to Congress for $1.2 billion in loan guarantees and was granted $1.5 billion, amid a great deal of controversy, as many Americans felt that it wasn't the government's place to lend money to a private company.

As it turned out, the gamble by Congress and Iacocca paid off. His economy cars—the K-cars—were a great success, espe-cially when Lee himself advertised them on television. By 1982 Chrysler was turning a modest profit again, and by 1983 it had actually managed to pay off its government debts ahead of sched-ule.

Lee's success at running Chrysler led to some suggestions that he run the whole country. But Lee squelched rumors that he might run for President in 1984. Instead, he wrote a bestselling autobiography and organized the highly successful restoration of the Statue of Liberty and the lavish celebration of its centennial on July 4, 1986.

Today, Lee remains at Chrysler—one of America's few cur-rent business celebrities.

THOMAS JEFFERSON

U.S. PRESIDENT, INVENTOR, ARCHITECT

BORN *Shadwell, Virginia, April 13, 1743*

DIED *Monticello, Virginia, July 4, 1826*

"We hold these truths to be self-evident; that all men are created equal . . ." There are perhaps no other words in American history more worthy of our respect than these from our Declaration of Independence. They were penned by Thomas Jefferson, our third President and a man whose life is a symbol of the American ideals of democracy and liberty.

Had he lived at another time, Thomas might have been a gentleman farmer or successful architect. Instead, he was a reluctant hero of the American Revolution—not on the bloody battlefield, but in the political and legal offices of a struggling new government.

Jefferson served his country in a variety of posts: in the Virginia legislature, as Governor of Virginia, Ambassador to France (where he cautiously advised French rebels in the course of their own Revolution), Vice President under John Adams, and President for two terms.

His achievements in these offices were vast: he devised a legal system for the state of Virginia and introduced the national coinage system we use today. His Bill for Establishing Religious Freedom formed an important foundation for the principle of separation of church and state, whereby church matters and government laws cannot infringe upon one another. As President, he virtually doubled the size of the United States with the shrewd purchase of the Louisiana territories. And always he fought for the rights of the poor and the working man against the tyranny of a privileged minority.

While politics provided him with a career, he was a man with diverse skills and interests. He was a mathematician, inventor, fiddle player, and architect. He designed and built his magnificent home, Monticello, as well as helping to design Washington, D.C., his nation's new capital.

After retiring from political life, he set about building the University of Virginia, a perfect monument of his love for learning and belief in democracy. To Jefferson, democracy—the rule of the people for the people—required learning for all. Without knowledge, he felt, there would be tyranny.

Although the exciting events of revolution drew him into public life, he was by nature a quiet, solitary man. He often said that he would rather be at home with his children, farming his estate, than in the fray of politics. He was a meticulous accountant, recording everything from blossoms in the garden to each penny he spent. And yet he died $100,000 in debt.

158

Perhaps his most disturbing contradiction was his stand on slavery. In principle, he despised it, feeling that it degraded everyone involved, master as well as slave. He felt trapped by an economy based on slave labor, fearing that his own Monticello could not survive without it. But he did, nevertheless, run his plantation by the labor of over 150 slaves. It was not until after his death, through a provision in his will, that some of his slaves were freed.

His private life, too, had an air of contradiction and mystery about it. Although a devoted husband to his wife Martha, his love life may not have ended with her death. While a subject of controversy, many modern historians now think that Thomas had a long and passionate affair with one of his slaves, Sally Hemmings, and had five children with her. And yet nowhere in Thomas's letters or journals is a single mention made of Sally or their children.

Today we can look with pride to the accomplishments of our third President, and consider his wisdom and courage as we continue to struggle with the responsibilities of democracy and liberty.

159

BUSTER KEATON

FILM STAR

BORN *Piqua, Kansas, October 4, 1895*

DIED *Hollywood, California, February 1, 1966*

Buster Keaton was both one of the funniest and one of the saddest men ever to grace American movie screens. Renowned for his little straw hat, his "great stone face," and his amazing stunts, his career as one of the greatest physical comedians of the silent film era was marked by personal tragedy.

Buster spent his childhood touring the United States with his parents, who were actors and acrobats in vaudeville—stage shows featuring many different acts, including acrobats, song and dance acts, and humorous skits. When Buster was born, his parents were working with the famous magician Harry Houdini. He was christened Joseph Frank, but was nicknamed Buster when he fell down a flight of stairs as a six-month-old baby and Houdini cried, "What a Buster!"

Buster soon got used to rough falls. He had joined his parents' act by the age of three, and they became very popular as "The Three Keatons." Like his father, Buster became adept at comic pratfalls, handsprings, and marksmanship.

By the time he was a teenager, Buster was the star of the act. But vaudeville was dying out, and his father was developing a drinking problem. When Buster was twenty-one, he and his mother were forced to stop working with him, fearing for their safety. Buster soon found new work in the short comic films of star Roscoe "Fatty" Arbuckle. He started out at $40 per week, but he proved so successful as a filmmaker and at the box office that he could afford to buy his own studio shortly after he got back from serving in World War I.

Buster wrote and directed most of his own movies, and never used a stunt double. An incredible athlete, he once dived seventy-five feet from a suspension bridge into a net. In the movie *College*, he pole-vaulted up into a second-floor window. In *Sherlock Jr.*, he rode a speeding motorcycle while sitting on the handlebars. And in *Steamboat Bill, Jr.*, Buster actually fractured his neck while twisting on his head for a scene during a cyclone. Somehow, he went on to finish the movie despite his injury.

The plots to most of Buster's movies were not very complicated. Usually, they were either takeoffs on popular films of the time or featured himself playing a ridiculous but determined underdog, fighting for respect and the hand of a female lead. His genius lay in inventing brilliant new twists to familiar comic situations, particularly chase scenes.

At the time, comic films were generally shorter than dramatic ones, but Buster's popularity helped lead to the first full-

161

length comic feature films. At the height of his career in the late 1920s, he was making $3,000 a week.

When soundtracks were added to movies, however, Buster's star faded fast. He made the mistake of giving up his own studio for a lucrative new contract with MGM, and soon lost artistic control of his films. Crushed by this and the breakup of his first marriage, Buster took to drinking heavily, and his Hollywood career looked bleak by the time he was forty.

Broke and almost desperate, Keaton was still able to battle back. He found work in Europe on the stage and in film. After a year of treatment, he triumphed over his alcoholism. Although he never again became a big star in Hollywood, he was able to get small parts on a regular basis.

In the 1950s and '60s, the first revivals of Buster's work were extremely popular and remain so to this day. Awarded a special Oscar in 1959 for his contributions to the art of cinema, Buster Keaton continued working in the art he loved up to the time of his death.

HELEN KELLER

WRITER, ADVOCATE FOR THE HANDICAPPED

BORN *Tuscumbia, Alabama, June 27, 1880*

DIED *Westport, Connecticut, June 1, 1968*

Helen Keller was a bright, smiling, happy child during her first eighteen months of life. But she took suddenly and dangerously ill with a raging fever that left her deaf, blind, and mute for the rest of her life. Despite these handicaps, this gifted woman became an international figure, respected as an author and advocate for the needs of handicapped people.

Helen's parents, Arthur and Kate, were devastated by their child's condition. Unsure of how to handle her, they let Helen grow into a wild, rough girl who screamed in frustration and rage.

Helen Keller and teacher Anne Sullivan

As unschooled as she was, however, Helen had independently developed her own form of language, which included sixty signs to indicate to those around her what she wanted. She made her family understand *her*.

Finally, after visiting countless doctors, the Keller family found a young woman, once partially blind herself, who would turn their daughter's life around. As immortalized in the famous William Gibson play and movie *The Miracle Worker*, Annie Sullivan was a patient, determined, and compassionate teacher who had studied at the renowned Perkins Institution for the Blind. She stayed with Helen until her own death almost fifty years later.

Annie taught Helen how to express herself using sign language to identify objects. Helen later revealed that the day she learned that every object, every feeling had its own name was "the most important day I remember in all my life." In a few months, she learned three hundred words and understood what they meant.

By the time she was eight, she had mastered Braille, a special kind of printing for the blind that uses raised dots on a page to symbolize letters. By touching these dots with their fingertips, blind people can read. At fourteen, after much pleading with her parents and Annie, Helen also learned to speak.

Always eager to test herself, to learn more, to try harder, Helen went to school at the age of fourteen, her beloved "Teacher," as she called Annie, spelling out lessons in sign language for her along the way.

In 1900, Helen entered Radcliffe College, the first woman so handicapped to do so. While still in school, she wrote her first autobiography, *Helen Keller: The Story of My Life*, with the aid of Annie's husband, literary critic John A. Macy.

With Macy's influence, Helen's active mind discovered a love of politics. Devoting herself to various social causes, she spoke out against racism and anti-Semitism and supported many liberal political candidates. She was also an ardent supporter of women's rights in the workplace and in the home.

More than any other issue, however, the plight of the handicapped was Helen's most important platform. Lecturing and writing continuously for support, she worked for various organizations devoted to that cause, including the American Foundation for the Blind and government agencies and commissions.

Tall, elegant, and with a quick sense of humor, Helen was a striking figure on her many travels throughout the United States and Europe. She was also a powerful writer of essays, autobiographies, inspirational books, and poetry. She received honorary degrees from many universities and was invited to the White House by every president from Grover Cleveland to John Kennedy. In 1964, President Johnson awarded her the Presidential Medal of Freedom.

Despite her great fame, Helen remained modest and down to earth, explaining "My life has been happy because I have had wonderful friends and plenty of interesting work to do. I seldom think about my limitations and they never make me sad. Perhaps there is just a touch of yearning at times, but it is vague, like a breeze among flowers. The wind passes, and the flowers are content." She died in 1968.

THE KENNEDY FAMILY

Perhaps no other American family in history has had as much influence on American politics and world affairs—or attracted as much publicity—as the Kennedys. Marked by tragedy, this dynasty of American politicians has nonetheless uniquely inspired a sense of optimism and purpose in the American people.

The patriarch of this wealthy and powerful family was Joseph Patrick Kennedy. Born in 1888, he was the son of a Boston tavernkeeper and Democratic community politician. Smart and aggressive, this Irish-Catholic boy was constantly rejected from the exclusively Protestant Boston clubs and businesses. But with a burning desire to be a millionaire before he was thirty-five, he defied them all. Shipbuilding, banking and even the motion-picture business helped to make him a fortune. When he put most of his money in the stock market, he made that work for him too.

Considered a business genius, he was named by President Franklin Roosevelt to the newly formed Securities and Exchange Commission in 1933. Four years later, Joe was appointed the first Irish-Catholic ambassador to Great Britain.

At home, he and his wife, Rose Fitzgerald, had nine children (Joe Jr., John, Rosemary, Kathleen, Eunice, Patricia, Robert, Jean, and Edward) to whom Joe was devoted. After growing up feeling the pains of discrimination, he wanted the very best for his children, especially his boys. Sending them to the best schools, he instilled in them his own driving ambition for power as well as a sense of public service and compassion.

Joe's real dream was to have his oldest son, Joe Jr., become the first Catholic President of the United States. But the first of many tragedies destroyed his hopes. Joe Jr. was killed in action during World War II. Kennedy's daughter Kathleen was later killed in a small plane accident in 1948.

And so it was left to John Fitzgerald Kennedy to take his father's ambitions and his own dreams into the White House. A dashing, handsome man with a beautiful wife, Jacqueline, John brought youth and intelligence to the most important job in the country. The Kennedy years of optimism were brought to a tragic end, however, when he was shot by an assassin in 1963.

The third Kennedy son, Robert, also involved himself in politics. Serving as his brother John's Attorney General, he was also New York's senator for three and a half years. During his campaign for President, he, too, was assassinated in June of 1968.

167

The last remaining Kennedy son, Edward, is senator from Massachusetts, a post he's held since 1962. Like his brothers before him, he has concentrated on social issues and liberal causes, including a national health insurance program and civil rights. And he too has had his share of personal tragedies. His son Ted Jr. suffered from bone cancer, requiring a leg to be amputated. Edward himself was involved in an accident in which a passenger in the car he was driving was killed.

The third generation of Kennedys is just now coming into its own. Joe Kennedy III, Robert's oldest son, is a member of Congress; Kathleen Kennedy Townsend, one of Robert's daughters, is a respected lawyer active in Maryland politics; Maria Shriver (daughter of Eunice Kennedy and Sargent Shriver) is a network news anchorwoman recently married to movie personality, Arnold Schwarzenegger, and Ted Jr. has become an active spokesperson for the handicapped.

Although several of the Kennedy children have had personal difficulties, including drug abuse, as a result of their fame and the high expectations placed on them by an adoring public, their 168 successes have brought the Kennedy dream of optimism and commitment to public service to yet another generation.

MARTIN LUTHER KING, JR.

CIVIL RIGHTS LEADER

BORN *Atlanta, Georgia, January 15, 1929*

DIED *Memphis, Tennessee, April 4, 1968*

"I have a dream that one day this nation will rise up and live out the true meaning of its creed: 'We hold these truths to be self-evident: that all men are created equal.' "

The Reverend Dr. Martin Luther King, Jr., spoke those words with compelling passion on August 28, 1963, on the steps of the Lincoln Memorial in Washington, D.C. Some 250,000 people had gathered to listen to this dynamic leader after taking part in the "March on Washington" to protest racism and discrimination against black Americans.

Martin Luther King, Jr., addressing crowd in Montgomery, Alabama, in 1956

The fight for civil rights is a struggle that continues today, and it was largely due to the efforts of this brave and inspired man that the civil rights movement in America first gained momentum.

Martin grew up in Atlanta, Georgia, the son of the Reverend Martin Luther King, Sr., pastor of the Ebenezer Baptist Church, and Alberta Williams King. Although Martin was raised in a warm and loving atmosphere, he couldn't help but see that black men were treated very badly in the white world. White people called his father "boy." Martin was forced to sit in the back of trolleys and buses and to give up his seat if a white person wanted it. More important, black men and women were kept from voting, one of the most sacred rights in American democracy.

Although he considered many different careers during high school and college, Martin decided that the best way to fight for justice would be to join the ministry. He graduated from college at the age of nineteen, then went on to study at Crozer Theological Seminary in Pennsylvania. He would later receive his Ph.D. from Boston University in 1955.

170 In the seminary, he studied the life of Mahatma Gandhi, the great Indian leader, and the writings of philosopher Henry David Thoreau, and gained greater understanding of the teachings of Christ. He learned that all of these men, true believers in nonviolence, also believed in civil disobedience—disobeying a law that they deeply believed was wrong and immoral. Martin saw this approach as a strategy for the American fight against racism.

He and his wife, Coretta Scott, moved to Montgomery, Alabama, where Martin took a position as pastor of the Dexter Avenue Baptist Church. It was in Montgomery that Martin Luther King's civil rights odyssey really began.

It would be a long and painful struggle, both in Montgomery and across the nation. In the years of protests, marches, boycotts, and sit-down strikes that followed, Martin Luther King led both black and white men and women to "the mountaintop of social justice." Their nonviolence was all too often met with tear gas, vicious bites from police dogs, beatings, lynchings, days in jail, and bombings.

Advances were made, however. On November 13, 1956, the Supreme Court declared that Alabama's bus segregation laws were unconstitutional. On July 2, 1964, after eight more years of persistent, nonviolent struggle, the Civil Rights Act of 1964 was signed by President Lyndon Johnson. It declared that black people had the same rights under the Constitution as white people, in the South as well as the North.

Later that year, Martin received international recognition for his courageous work when he won the Nobel Peace Prize—the youngest, at thirty-five, ever to do so, and only the second black American.

But his work was not over. Although laws had been changed, people's attitudes had not. Martin continued to use his great skills as a compelling speaker and his dynamic personality to bring this to the attention of America and the world.

On April 4, 1968, Martin was preparing a protest in support 171 of striking sanitation workers in Memphis, Tennessee, and a Poor People's March to Washington, D.C. later in the year. As he stood on the balcony of his motel room, a shot rang out. A lone assassin had used a bullet to kill a man whose dream had been to bring peace and justice to America.

DOROTHEA LANGE

PHOTOGRAPHER

BORN *Hoboken, New Jersey, May 26, 1895*

DIED *Berkeley, California, October 11, 1965*

Dorothea Lange was one of the world's great artists and a chronicler of one of America's most difficult times in history, the Great Depression. Dorothea used her skill with a camera to document the effects of poverty and despair in the faces of young and old Americans—transforming journalistic photos into art.

Dorothea's sensitivity to others' pain may have stemmed from the fact that her own life was not an easy one. Her father, whom she adored, left home without warning when she was just twelve years old. She never saw or heard from him again. Another difficulty Dorothea encountered was a crippling bout with polio. She was ill for over a year and was left with a limp. While her mother, Joan Lange, loved her only daughter, she was often insensitive to Dorothea's discomfort about her lameness and seemed embarrassed that Dorothea couldn't walk normally. It was an attitude that Dorothea would never forget.

Joan worked as a librarian on Manhattan's Lower East Side, across the Hudson from their small home in Hoboken, New Jersey. Every day she took her daughter to a school near the library, but although Dorothea was a bright and inquisitive child, she never liked school very much. She preferred being on her own, outside in the crowded streets. Soon she skipped school whenever she could.

As Dorothea walked through the streets of the neighborhood, she saw the down-and-out alcoholics sleeping on the streets of the Bowery and the dirty-faced children playing outside broken-down tenements. She drank in every detail of the things she saw; she devoured people's smiles and stances the way others gobbled up books or baseball games. Dorothea took every chance she had to visit museums and galleries to study paintings and photographs. By the time Dorothea graduated from high school, she knew she wanted to be a photographer, without ever having held a camera in her hand.

173

One day, while on one of her walks through the streets of Manhattan she came upon the studio of the master photographer, Arnold Genthe. Without planning what she would say about her lack of experience with a camera, she went in and asked Mr. Genthe for a job. Exactly what made him hire her is unknown, but he gave Dorothea her first job in what would be a life-long career. Finally, she could hold a camera up to her gifted eye and snap away.

Learning as much as she could about the technical aspects of photography from Genthe and others, Dorothea began to develop her own style. Soon she moved to San Francisco, where she opened her own portrait studio. In 1920, she married painter Maynard Dixon with whom she had two sons. For the next nine years, when the United States was in an economic upswing, many wealthy San Franciscans hired Dorothea to photograph them.

Then, on October 29, 1929, the stock market crashed and the country was plunged into the Depression. Millions of men and women were out of work. People lost their homes, their farms, their dignity. Times were rough for Dorothea as well, since photographs were now luxuries few could afford. Memories of the faces she had seen during her childhood inspired her to leave the studio and take her camera into the streets once again.

Throughout the 1930s, Dorothea documented the tragedy of the Great Depression in the faces of Californians and the thousands of migrant workers who came there looking for work. She had already met Paul Taylor, a college professor with whom she formed a partnership. After being hired by the U.S. Government to document the Depression, Dorothea and Paul created an unforgettable portrait, not just of the unique individuals who struggled every day to survive, but of the entire nation. Their partnership grew into love, and having divorced her first husband in 1924, Dorothea married Paul.

174

When the Depression was over, they continued their work. During World War II, Dorothea was asked by the United States Government to photograph the Japanese-American internment camps, where millions of American citizens of Japanese descent were imprisoned until the war was over. It was only in 1972 that these photographs were published and put on display.

Dorothea lived a long and in some ways difficult life. Her work caused her to leave her children with foster families and relatives while she and her husband traveled, an arrangement that caused her immeasurable pain. She was ill for much of her later life, with ulcers and then with cancer. She died in 1965. Today, her photographs, especially "White Angel Breadline" and "Migrant Mother," are considered unequaled works of art.

NORMAN LEAR

MOTION PICTURE AND
TELEVISION PRODUCER

BORN *New Haven, Connecticut, July 27, 1922*

From "All in the Family" to "Maude" to "Mary Hartman, Mary Hartman," Norman Lear has provided American television audiences with some of the most innovative material in the history of television. Written with an eye toward both comedy and social commentary, these shows and others in the Norman Lear portfolio challenge American views on race relations, the Vietnam War, women's rights, and other controversial issues.

Norman has a quiet and gentle manner that surprises many people who expect the producer of such outrageous comedy to be more outrageous himself. But Norman is serious about humor, dedicated to enlightening his audiences. He once told a reporter, "I want to entertain, but I gravitate to subjects that matter and people worth caring about."

Memories of his own childhood in a lower-middle-class family in New Haven provided Norman with inspiration for some shows, especially for "All in the Family." Herman Lear, Norman's father, was a rather intolerant man, treating his family with disdain, telling his wife to "stifle herself" and calling Norman "the laziest white kid I ever saw,"—remarks Archie Bunker, the central character in "All in the Family," would make with great frequency to his own household.

Norman's career in show business began in 1949, when he and a friend, Ed Simmons, wrote a comedy skit that entertainer Danny Thomas bought and used during a Hollywood benefit. After that, he and Simmons were hired to write for one regular television series after another, including "The Colgate Comedy Hour," which starred Dean Martin and Jerry Lewis.

Bud Yorkin, then associate director of "The Colgate Comedy Hour," and Norman became friends and formed a production company of their own, Tandem Productions, Inc., in 1959. With Norman and Bud alternately writing, directing and producing, Tandem produced such hit movies of the 1960s as *Come Blow Your Horn, Never Too Late,* and *Divorce, American Style,* for which Norman won an Academy Award nomination for Best Screenplay.

It was, however, in television that Norman and his partner's talents were best served. Adapting a British comedy about a bigoted working-class man and his liberal son for American audiences and adding in many of his childhood memories, he created "All in the Family." Dealing with issues that had never received the kind of prime-time exposure this show would offer, "All in the Family" questioned American attitudes on a number of social issues.

176

While not an immediate success, by the end of its first season in 1971 "All in the Family" had become the most popular show on the air, averaging sixty million viewers every week. In just two seasons it earned seven Emmys and by the time it went off the air in 1979, the show and its stars, Carroll O'Connor, Jean Stapleton, Sally Struthers, and Rob Reiner had racked up an astounding seventeen Emmys.

"All in the Family" spawned many successful spin-offs, including "Maude," "Good Times," and "The Jeffersons." In addition to Tandem Productions, Norman formed his own company, T.A.T. Productions, from which came such hits as "One Day at a Time," "Hot L Baltimore," and the late-night soap opera spoof, "Mary Hartman, Mary Hartman." With sixteen television series produced in the 1970s alone—many of which are still aired before wide audiences—Norman Lear has made an extraordinary contribution to television.

ROBERT E. LEE

SOLDIER

BORN *Stratford, Virginia, January 19, 1807*

DIED *Lexington, Virginia, October 12, 1870*

A ruthlessly brilliant general, Robert E. Lee has endured as an American military hero despite his support for the lost Confederate cause during the Civil War.

Born into one of the oldest and most distinguished families of Virginia, Robert had three heroes in his own family—two of his cousins had signed the Declaration of Independence and his father, Henry "Light-Horse Harry" Lee, had been a famous Revolutionary War general.

Robert's childhood, however, was difficult. His father lost

most of the family's money through bad investments and died when Robert was only eleven. His mother was often ill. But Robert studied hard in school and was able to get into the United States Military Academy at West Point, graduating second in his class.

For the next seventeen years in his lifelong career in the army, Robert was given a number of different assignments, including strengthening military forts around the country, overseeing Mississippi River flood control projects, and examining Atlantic coastal defenses. As part of the invasion force during the Mexican War, Robert fought well and received a commendation for his daring tactics and efficient work. One of his fellow officers in the war was Ulysses S. Grant, who would later prove to be a formidable enemy.

After the Mexican War, Robert, now a colonel, put in three years as superintendent of his old school, West Point. When his home state of Virginia seceded in 1861 at the start of the Civil War, however, he resigned his commission and joined the Confederate Army.

Slavery was the major issue that separated the Confederates (Southerners) from the Union Army (Northerners) and Robert's dilemma was that of many men at the time. While he owned a female slave and her children, he did not particularly support the institution of slavery. He did, however, put loyalty to his home state above loyalty to the nation. 179

Robert's military expertise was great. When he took command of the Army of Northern Virginia in 1862, he had to face a much larger Union force trying to capture the Confederate capital of Richmond, Virginia. Robert surprised the Union forces by anticipating their every move. It was the first major victory for the tall, dignified man with the trim white beard.

His men adored him, and with their help and that of his equally legendary second-in-command, Thomas "Stonewall" Jackson, Robert fought bravely against the Northern forces. But his efforts could not stem the Union tide. Union armies were scoring repeated victories in the western part of the Confederacy. The Union blockade of Confederate ports cut off needed supplies and the North had a huge advantage in men and resources.

Robert was forced into a desperate strategy of attacking the North, which ended in disaster. At Antietam, his forces were devastated by the North in the bloodiest single day of combat ever fought in the Western Hemisphere. The second time he invaded the North, he was defeated at Gettysburg and the tide of the war turned.

Lincoln then appointed General Grant to command the Union armies. Grant pursued Lee in a long series of battles designed to wear down the Confederacy. Although Robert's brilliant tactics long held the North at bay, by mid-1864 Grant had Richmond under siege, and the Confederates were finally forced to surrender in April of 1865.

After the war, Robert became president of Washington College in Virginia, later renamed Washington and Lee. Long after his death in 1870, Robert E. Lee's legacy lives on, as a great hero of the Confederacy, a man who fought a losing cause with courage.

ABRAHAM LINCOLN

PRESIDENT

BORN *Near Hodgenville, Kentucky, February 12, 1809*
DIED *Washington, D.C., April 15, 1865*

"A house divided against itself cannot stand. I believe this government cannot endure, permanently half *slave* and half *free.*" During one of the most violent and difficult times in our history, Abraham Lincoln devoted himself to ensuring that America did endure as one nation.

Abraham experienced a hard frontier life as a boy. His father eked out a living as a carpenter and farmer, and his mother died when he was only a young boy. Like so many frontier children, he was needed to work at home and was only able to get a few years of schooling. He grew to be a tall, lanky young man, six feet, four inches tall, with a homely but striking face and powerful muscles from splitting wooden rails.

While running a general store, Abe studied to become a lawyer. He then went into politics, eventually winning eight years in the Illinois state legislature, and then a seat in the House of Representatives, which he held for one term.

For the next ten years, Abe won fame and respect as a lawyer. At that time in America's frontier towns, lawyers and judges alike had to travel many miles to try cases, sleeping in overcrowded hotels. But the sociable Abe enjoyed the chance to meet people, and became an expert storyteller.

It was during this time that Abe met Mary Todd, whom he would later marry. Although they loved each other, the marriage would be difficult. Mary's mental stability deteriorated as two of her four children died before they reached eighteen years of age.

By 1858, the country was badly divided over the issue of slavery. Abe had joined the new Republican Party, a group of anti-slavery organizations. At that time, Abe did not believe that freeing the slaves was worth a civil war, and he even proposed that American blacks be resettled in Africa and Central America, because he believed they would never be treated well by white Americans.

But he did oppose the institution of slavery on moral grounds, and was against extending the practice to the many new states joining the Union. He argued this viewpoint against Stephen Douglas when the two men ran against each other for the U.S. Senate, in perhaps the greatest series of debates ever waged by two American politicians. Douglas won that election, but Abe beat him in the presidential election of 1860.

Unfortunately, the Southern states refused to accept any limits on slavery and seceded from the Union to form the

Confederate States of America. America was plunged into the Civil War.

It would be a difficult and bloody struggle. The South had most of the ablest generals, Lincoln had almost no standing army to fight with, and many Northerners were opposed to the war. But Abe, as Commander in Chief, persisted. In 1863, he issued the Emancipation Proclamation, formally freeing all slaves.

In 1863, Abe, a brilliant public speaker, made his famous Gettysburg Address at the site of a crucial Union victory. Proclaiming again his devotion to a nation "conceived in liberty and dedicated to the proposition that all men are created equal," he moved the crowd and signaled his determination to unite his divided nation. Slowly but surely, Lincoln was able to utilize the North's vast superiority in men and resources. In 1864, a wave of Union victories assured his reelection.

Abe lived to see the North win the war. A few days later, on Good Friday, 1865, he was assassinated by a deranged actor while attending a play. When his body was carried back to Illinois by train, people lined the rails for miles to pay their final respects to "the Great Emancipator." 183

CHARLES A. LINDBERGH, JR.

AVIATOR

BORN *Detroit, Michigan, February 4, 1902*

DIED *Kipahulu, Maui, Hawaii, August 26, 1974*

On May 20, 1927, Charles Lindbergh embarked on one of the most famous journeys in history. Backed by several St. Louis bankers and civic leaders, this twenty-five-year-old aviator made the first nonstop flight from New York to Paris. After taking off from Roosevelt Field on Long Island, New York, in his monoplane (a plane with just one set of wings) *The Spirit of St. Louis,* he flew the long and arduous flight alone, landing in Paris 33½ hours later, a national hero and international celebrity.

Aviation had been Charles's passion ever since he first

caught a glimpse of a plane in 1912 in Washington, D.C., where his father had moved after being elected a U.S. Representative from Minnesota. An average, if restless, student, Charles attended a number of different grammar and high schools, both public and private. He graduated from Little Falls High School in 1918. Deciding to give college a try, Charles entered the University of Wisconsin, where he became a member of the Reserve Officers Training Corps. He lost interest in his studies, however, admitting he found them "irksome." He left college to enter a flying school conducted by the Nebraska Aircraft Company in Lincoln, Nebraska.

After less than two months of instruction, he helped another aviator, E. G. Bahl, on a barnstorming trip, during which they performed stunts in the air for passengers who paid five dollars apiece for a ten-minute ride. Charles continued to work as a stunt flier, both with Bahl and the famous stunt pilot Charles Harden, with whom he made a double parachute jump. He took his first solo trip in April 1923, after buying a U.S. surplus wartime plane from the government for $500. In 1924, he enrolled at Brooks Field, San Antonio, Texas, as a flying cadet in the United States   185
Air Service to continue his career as an aviator.

According to his autobiography, Charles first thought of trying a transatlantic flight after hearing about a $25,000 prize offered by hotel magnate Raymond Ortieg for the first nonstop flight from New York to Paris. Using his charm and enthusiasm as bait, Charles persuaded a group of civic-minded St. Louis businessmen to give him financial backing and purchase an appropriate plane for the trip. The story of the incredible flight that followed was told by Charles Lindbergh himself in *The Spirit of St. Louis,* for which he won a Pulitzer Prize.

Charles's flying days, however, were hardly over. He was just twenty-five years old, and for nearly fifty more years would distinguish himself as an expert aviator in both civilian and military life. In December of 1927, he arrived in Mexico City from Washington after a twenty-seven-hour flight, and at a reception there in his honor he met Anne Spencer Morrow, whom he married in 1929. During the first years of their marriage, the Lindberghs made numerous flights together to various parts of the globe. They were one of the most famous couples in America; their fame and popularity were unrivaled.

Their happy world was shattered, however, in 1932 when their almost two-year-old son was kidnapped. The whole world waited in horror while the police searched in vain for the missing child, who was later found murdered. The publicity was overwhelming—it was deemed "the crime of the century" and the man convicted of the crime, Bruno Hauptmann, was executed.

The Lindberghs moved to Europe in 1935, perhaps to avoid even more public scrutiny. Charles was able to survey German air power and make significant reports to the U.S. government concerning Hitler's rise to power and subsequent remilitarization of Germany. Back in the United States, Charles was a leading isolationist, campaigning against the involvement of the United States in the war brewing in Europe and the Pacific. After President Roosevelt criticized his behavior, Charles resigned his colonel's commission in the Army Air Corps.

186

Despite his reluctance, once Pearl Harbor was bombed by the Japanese and America officially declared war, Charles joined the American effort as a civilian consultant hired by the Ford Motor Company and the United Aircraft Company. He would also accompany fifty combat missions in the Pacific Theater for the U.S. military. For his brave and dedicated service during World War II and after, when he went to Germany once again to survey their aircraft, his commission in the Armed Forces was reinstated by President Eisenhower. Later, he was named brigadier general in the Air Force Reserve.

Throughout the rest of his life, he worked as a consultant for the U.S. Defense Department and for Pan American World Airways. He wrote extensively, mainly autobiographical works, and his wife Anne was also a writer of note. The intense publicity that attended the couple during their time of glory and tragedy had made them very private—some say aloof—people. They lived quiet lives, in Darien, Connecticut, and in Hawaii until Charles died in 1974.

CLARE BOOTHE LUCE

WRITER, CONGRESSWOMAN, AMBASSADOR

BORN *New York, New York, April 10, 1903*

DIED *Washington, D.C., October 9, 1987*

Clare Boothe Luce, actress, magazine editor, Broadway playwright, war correspondent, congresswoman, and ambassador, has achieved more in a lifetime than most of us can imagine.

She was born into a cultured but poverty-stricken family. Clare's father was a violinist who deserted his wife when Clare was a small child. Her mother, Ann, was determined that her child would not lack either comfort or social respectability. Thanks to a friendship with a wealthy and generous merchant named Joseph Jacobs, Ann was able to educate her daughter in private finishing schools in Memphis, Chicago and, for a year, in France.

After graduating from Miss Mason's School in 1919, Clare decided to take a stab at the theatrical world, studying at a theater school in New York. Later that year her mother and stepfather took her on a trip to Europe, where she met George Tuttle Brokaw, a millionaire whom she married in 1923. Only twenty at the time, Clare spent six years in an unhappy marriage that finally ended in divorce.

Left with a small daughter of her own, Clare was forced to support herself. Although with few qualifications, she managed to land a position first at *Vogue* magazine and then at *Vanity Fair* magazine, a well-respected publication employing some of the best writers of the day. She started out writing captions for photographs, but was made associate editor within a year and managing editor three years later, in 1933.

In 1935 Clare married Henry Luce, a wealthy magazine publisher and founder of *Time* magazine. Eventually Clare left *Vanity Fair*, first to write for the Broadway stage, a career she pursued for many years. *The Women, Kiss the Boys Goodbye,* and *Margin for Error* were three of her biggest hits. *The Women* was twice made into a movie.

Bored with theater despite her success, Clare turned her energies to her husband's growing empire, especially the creation of *Life* magazine, an innovative, photograph-filled journal. Visiting war-torn Europe after the start of World War II as a correspondent for *Life,* Clare interviewed some of the most influential world leaders of the day.

Back home, Clare explored another of her many interests— politics. Although she initially supported President Roosevelt's foreign policy of the late 1930s, she turned against him and campaigned for unsuccessful Republican candidate Wendell Willkie in the 1940 presidential election. When her only daugh-

189

ter, Ann, was killed in a car accident in 1944, an emotionally devastated Clare poured even more of herself into her new career in politics.

Finding the perfect political arena for her sensibilities and talents, Clare herself ran for Congress and won. During her four years in office, Clare was often in the headlines with speeches critical of President Roosevelt and his administration, and later of President Truman.

While in Congress, Clare was known as a vocal anti-Communist. She introduced or supported a number of bills, including one to acknowledge U.S. responsibility for the surrender of Poland to the Soviet Union. Generally conservative in international relations, Clare was more progressive domestically. She supported women's rights and introduced a bill to establish equal pay for equal work, regardless of race, color, or creed.

In 1952 Clare lost a campaign for the Republican nomination for Senator from Connecticut. But as a reward for her vigorous support of Dwight Eisenhower's presidential campaign, she was named Ambassador to Italy—only the second American woman ambassador in history. She served in Rome for four years and then was nominated to serve as Ambassador to Brazil. This nomination was met with opposition from the Senate, which has the power to block the President's choices for certain government posts. Dismayed by the treatment she had received, Clare resigned before serving in the post.

Clare kept a high profile in Republican politics until her death in 1987. She campaigned to elect Barry Goldwater to the presidency in 1964, and in 1982 and 1983 served on President Reagan's Foreign Intelligence Board. In 1983 she received the Presidential Medal of Freedom, a fitting reward for a woman who devoted her life to public service.

DOUGLAS
MacARTHUR

MILITARY LEADER

BORN *Little Rock, Arkansas, January 26, 1880*

DIED *Washington, D.C., April 5, 1964*

Douglas MacArthur was a controversial figure in United States history. Considered one of the greatest military leaders of the twentieth century, Douglas MacArthur inspired the loyalty and admiration of those who served him despite, or perhaps because of, a singlemindedness that would cause one American President to strip him of his rank. His handsome six-foot frame and commanding demeanor, however, came to symbolize the greatness of American military power and strength.

The son of Captain Arthur MacArthur and his wife Mary

Hardy, Douglas was born in the Government Armory Building at Little Rock Barracks in Arkansas while his father was fighting Indians on the new Western frontier. Raised on military posts and witnessing with pride the accomplishments of his father, Douglas could never imagine any career but service to his country.

Douglas never experienced the ordinary school life of most children, but proved himself to be an extremely bright young man when he entered the Texas Military Institute at the age of thirteen.

It was no surprise to his family, then, that Douglas scored 700 out of 750 points on the entrance examination for the West Point Military Academy, or that he graduated first in his class four years later. He graduated as a second lieutenant and first served under his father's leadership in the Orient.

From then on, his career was marked by distinguished appointments and service. During World War I, Douglas fought courageously as a commander in France. He received two Purple Hearts and was cited ten more times for extreme bravery under fire. By the time the war was over, he had been promoted to the rank of general and became the youngest division commander in the U.S. Army.

Back home after the war, Douglas took charge of West Point, where he modernized the Academy, sometimes against the opposition of its academic board. His independence and stubbornness were resented, but even those who found his unorthodox behavior troublesome recognized his brilliant mind and moral integrity.

During the next nineteen years, until the Americans entered World War II, MacArthur helped the country modernize its military capabilities, anticipating the threat of Japanese and German militarization. In 1935 he returned to the Philippines to head the American military mission there, serving to establish a Philippine Military Academy and modernize the republic's armed forces.

MacArthur was in the Philippines when Pearl Harbor was

bombed and the United States entered World War II. After being made Commander of the U.S. forces in the Far East, he was ordered to leave his post for Australia. But before departing, he uttered some of the most famous words of the war, "I shall return," promising never to desert the country he'd served so well. It took more than two years, but MacArthur did return to lead his troops in the liberation of the Philippines from the Japanese.

Eventually made a five-star General of the Army, MacArthur commanded the Allied forces in the Southwest Pacific. The Japanese surrendered on August 15, 1945. For the next five years, as supreme commander for the Allied Powers, MacArthur attempted to reform many of Japan's social and political traditions.

Douglas was again called into active duty during the Korean War. He was relieved of his command by President Truman, however, after publicly disagreeing with the President's policies. Fearing the Chinese Communist threat, Douglas wanted to expand the war into China, which was against U.S. policy.

Despite this rather inglorious end to a distinguished military career, MacArthur was met with grand receptions and parades back home in the States. A staunch Republican, he unsuccessfully tried to win the presidential nomination in 1944, 1948, and 1952. He served as chairman of the board of Remington Rand (later Sperry-Rand) Corporation until his retirement. He died in 1964 at the age of eighty-four.

JOHN McENROE

TENNIS PLAYER

BORN *Wiesbaden, West Germany, February 16, 1959*

At the peak of his game, John McEnroe was one of the best players in the history of professional tennis. Throughout his career, his intense concentration and athletic ability have been matched only by his on-court antics.

From the time he was a young boy, John showed remarkable athletic prowess and ambition. John had many opportunities to compete with his two brothers, Patrick and Mark, in school, on the tennis court, and in other sports. Even then he was very competitive. His father recently told a reporter, "John *always* wanted to win."

His father, John McEnroe, Sr., has been his manager since the beginning of his career. He and his wife, Kay, have both been constant supporters of John's career, despite his outrageous temper and competitive streak. "The signs were always there," Kay told an *Esquire* magazine reporter. "If he didn't get the best mark in Latin, even in grammar school, he'd be *furious.*"

Although John displayed amazing talents as a basketball and soccer player in high school, his father steered him toward tennis. Concentrating on tennis, John won numerous junior titles, was the youngest player at that time to reach the semifinals at Wimbledon in 1977, won the French mixed doubles in 1977, and took the National Collegiate Athletic Association singles men's title in 1978.

Later that same year, after his freshman year at Stanford University, he turned professional. Taking the tennis world by storm, he won several major international tournaments and was a member of the champion United States Davis Cup team.

From the beginning, John's strength as a tennis player has been his incredible racket control and creativity. While his serve is powerful, his real talent lies in his ability to move to the net with lightning speed, surprising his opponents by returning nearly impossible shots. He also thrills fans of the game with his artistic array of drop and touch shots, carefully hitting the ball just where his opponent can't reach it.

As exciting as John's actual game of tennis has been to watch, it just barely measures up to the temper tantrums he has displayed on and off the court. Highlights of major tournaments almost always feature John flinging racquets, arguing with the linesmen, gesturing, and swearing. Officials, photographers, fans, and even his opponents have felt his wrath and he has been fined large sums of money for his frequent outbursts.

In the late 1970s and early 1980s, John slowly came to dominate men's tennis, taking the number-one spot away from the

195

great Swedish star Björn Borg. Their athletic styles were a study in contrasts, with Borg always dignified, quiet, and reserved. Their rivalry was legendary.

At first Borg usually won, but after he defeated John in an epic 1980 Wimbledon match the tide began to turn. That same year, John stopped Borg's bid for a Grand Slam (winning the Australian, French, U.S., and Wimbledon opens) by beating him in a thrilling U.S. Open final.

The win gave John the second of his three straight U.S. titles. He also took the Wimbledon singles title in 1981, 1983, and 1984, won the World Tennis Championship in 1979, 1981, and 1983 and has won many doubles titles.

With Borg's retirement, it looked as if John might have a long reign as champion. But the loss of his old rival seemed to take a bit of the thrill out of tennis for him, and new champions like Ivan Lendl and Boris Becker proved to be challenging opponents. After his highly publicized marriage to actress Tatum O'Neal, John took nearly a year off when they had their first child, Kevin Jack. The couple now have a second son, Sean.

196 Since his return to tennis in 1986, John seems to lack his former concentration and is generally eliminated early in tournaments. "I gotta believe I can do it again," he recently told a reporter. "I'm not going to panic if I lose some matches . . . I'm going to be around for a while." Still barely thirty years old, it remains to be seen whether he'll reach his former peak. But he will certainly go down in tennis history as a true master of the game.

MARGARET MEAD

ANTHROPOLOGIST

BORN *Philadelphia, Pennsylvania, December 16, 1901*

DIED *New York, New York, November 15, 1978*

"The way in which each human infant is transformed into the finished adult, into the complicated individual version of his city and his century is one of the most fascinating studies open to the curious-minded," Margaret Mead once wrote. Like no other scientist, she made the study of human history and behavior—anthropology—a part of the way we all look at contemporary society.

Despite growing up at a time when career choices were rather limited for young women, Margaret was determined to study primitive cultures in sometimes faraway and dangerous lands. Ignoring those who said that such expeditions were "a man's work," she undertook some of the most innovative and meaningful anthropological work of the twentieth century.

Margaret was brought up in Philadelphia, where her father taught economics at the University of Pennsylvania and her mother was a sociologist. Her grandmother, Martha Ramsay Mead, an early pioneer of child psychology, taught her granddaughter to take notes on the behavior of younger children when Margaret herself was only eight years old. Although Margaret once considered becoming a painter, her family's concentration on the social sciences influenced her greatly.

Margaret majored in English and psychology at Barnard College. After studying under two renowned scientists, Professor Franz Boas and Dr. Ruth Benedict, Margaret decided to make anthropology her career. Their theories centered on the idea that the personality of each human being is directly related to the society and culture in which he or she lives, rather than heredity or biological factors. Proving this became the motivation for Margaret's own work.

In 1925, Margaret embarked on her first field expedition— to study adolescent girls in a primitive tribe in Samoa, a group of islands in the South Pacific. She immersed herself in their culture, adopting Samoan dress and learning native dances while scrupulously taking notes on everything she observed about the way young Samoan girls grew up.

Upon her return to the United States nearly a year later, Margaret published her findings in a remarkable book, *Coming of Age in Samoa.* In it, Margaret observed that what was considered "typical" teenage behavior—emotional outbursts, showing off, and general stress-related reactions—weren't experienced in Samoa. Young girls went through puberty calmly, with a maturity rarely seen in the West. This prompted Margaret to conclude that behavior was directly influenced by society. Stress in American teens, therefore, came mostly from the way they learned to act from their parents and other adults, not only from the biological changes that take place during puberty.

Margaret's study was considered ground-breaking work, and her findings were largely accepted by the scientific establishment. It brought her international acclaim, as well as the prestigious job of Assistant Curator, later Curator, of Ethnology at the Museum of Natural History in New York. The book also proved her to be an excellent writer, able to describe complicated and intense experiences to readers in an accessible, sensitive way. She authored over twenty books and hundreds of scientific papers and articles during her long, active life.

Margaret was just twenty-five when she returned from Samoa, and she would work for the next fifty years as a dedicated anthropologist. Field work would take her all over the world and her findings would attract larger and larger audiences. She was outspoken about contemporary social issues, too, always drawing upon her scientific experience to analyze current events. As she wrote in her critically acclaimed autobiography, *Blackberry Winter,* "I have spent most of my life studying the lives of other peoples, faraway peoples, so that Americans might better understand themselves."

RALPH NADER

CONSUMER ACTIVIST

B O R N *Winsted, Connecticut, February 27, 1934*

Padded steering wheels and dashboards, pollution-control exhaust systems, mandatory safety belts—these are a few of the automobile safety features Americans take for granted today. But it wasn't until one young crusader named Ralph Nader put the automobile industry on trial with his bestselling book *Unsafe at Any Speed* in 1965 that the rights of consumers were taken seriously.

A man of vision and integrity, Ralph Nader remains the symbol of the consumer rights movement today. Believing that most large corporations have little regard for the safety or health of individual consumers, he has worked with Congress to enact laws to force corporations to live up to certain standards. His efforts have resulted in laws to protect us against unsafe water and food, dangerous working conditions, and defective products. Most important, thanks to the attention Ralph brought to these issues there are now city, state, and federal consumer affairs agencies to which the average consumer can go for help.

Ralph grew up learning the importance of the justice system from his parents, Nadra and Rose Nader, Lebanese immigrants. His father, a restaurant owner in the small town of Winsted, Connecticut, once told a reporter that Ralph had been brought up to "understand that working for justice in this country is a safeguard of our democracy." It was a lesson Ralph took to heart. At the age of four, he was already hanging around courthouses listening to lawyers argue cases, and dreaming of a law career himself.

On scholarship to Princeton University, Ralph began his crusade against what he considers to be negligence and greed on the part of large corporations, manufacturers, and even universities. At Princeton, for instance, he campaigned to prevent the administration from having trees on campus sprayed with DDT, a dangerous pesticide later banned from use.

After graduating, Ralph went on to receive his law degree at Harvard University. It was there that he first became interested in auto safety issues. While studying auto injury cases, he found that unsafe vehicle design caused far more accidents than did driver error. The fact that the auto industry was never held accountable for faulty designs that caused countless deaths and injuries inflamed Ralph's sense of justice.

Before arriving in Washington, D.C., to take on the automobile industry, Ralph served six months in the army, traveled in Latin America, Europe, and Africa as a free-lance journalist, then worked in a private law practice in Hartford, Connecticut. After two years of campaigning for auto safety on the local level, Ralph decided to take his fight to the nation's capital in 1964.

Working first for the Labor Department on an auto safety study, Ralph then left the government to write his own book, *Unsafe at Any Speed*. He testified at a number of congressional hearings until the National Traffic and Motor Vehicle Safety Act of 1966—the first of many laws he would introduce—was passed by Congress and signed into law by President Lyndon Johnson.

In the over twenty years since, Ralph has continued to work on behalf of the consumer in a number of different industries. At the heart of his philosophy is the belief in the responsibility of each individual to take part in public affairs. To that end, he inspired the creation of a number of public affairs organizations, including Public Interest Research Groups (PIRGs). Run by young activists nicknamed "Nader's Raiders," PIRGs have sponsored consumer legislation in Washington and in some twenty-six states throughout the nation.

Ralph's busy schedule allows little time for a social life, and he has never married. He lives in Washington, D.C., does not own a car, and reportedly spends very little money on clothes or other personal belongings.

JOE NAMATH

FOOTBALL PLAYER, BROADCASTER

BORN *Beaver Falls, Pennsylvania, May 31, 1943*

Few athletes have received as much popular support and notoriety on and off the playing field as Joe Namath, considered one of the best quarterbacks in the history of American football. For over ten seasons with the New York Jets, Joe Namath was the top box-office drawing card in the American Football League.

Joe grew up in the steel mill town of Beaver Falls, Pennsylvania. His father, Frank Namath, was a steel mill worker who had immigrated from Hungary. When Joe was in sixth grade, his parents divorced, and he and his four siblings were brought up by his mother, Rose.

Joe was a natural athlete, introduced to football by his older brothers when he was only five. Even then, he threw a ball with such precision that he could, as his mother recalled to a reporter, "hit a stump forty yards away." Baseball, too, was an abiding passion and he started Little League baseball at age six.

In high school Joe starred in football, baseball, and basketball, and in his senior year was inundated with offers from colleges and major league baseball teams. Although baseball was his greatest love, he decided to get a college education on a football scholarship.

At the University of Alabama, Joe's talent as a player was fully realized. His remarkably strong throwing arm and uncanny ability to see through an opposing team's defenses made him the perfect quarterback. In his sophomore year he guided his team to a record of ten wins in eleven games.

In his senior season, Joe's right knee was injured for the first time when it collapsed under him as he came to an abrupt stop during a play. Bearing the brunt of a rough contact sport, under constant strain of sudden moves and the impact of tackles, Joe's knees would trouble him throughout his career.

Considered by professional teams to be one of the best catches in 1965, Joe decided to leave college one semester before graduation to sign with the New York Jets. Teams from both the American League and the National League had vied for this talented newcomer, but Joe signed with the New York Jets, an American Football League team, when he was offered nearly $400,000 and a Lincoln Continental for a three-year contract.

The American Football League, having played second fiddle to the more powerful National Football League, needed a strong star to help them toward victory and draw fans. In Joe, they found their star. His greatest moment came in the 1969 Super Bowl Game in which the Jets played the Baltimore Colts. Determined to be the first AFL team to win the Super Bowl, the Jets played hard and Joe perhaps hardest of all. Completing 17 out of 28 passes and reading the Colt defenses superbly, he led his team to a stunning 16–7 victory.

Joe's handsome six-foot-two frame, winning smile, and reputation as a ladies' man earned him the nickname "Broadway Joe." The toast of New York's hottest discos, Joe's freewheeling lifestyle had his name popping up in gossip columns almost as often as on sports pages.

After retiring from football in 1978, Joe decided to put his good looks, charm, and ability to work as an actor. Movies, commercials, and even stage plays in regional theaters have kept him active and in the public spotlight. Now happily married and the father of a young daughter, Joe has put his flashy lifestyle and acting career behind him. But he can still be seen and heard on NBC television as a sports announcer for NFL games.

ANNIE OAKLEY

SHARPSHOOTER, PERFORMER

BORN *Darke County, Ohio, August 13, 1860*

DIED *Greenville, Ohio, November 2, 1926*

At thirty paces and with her favorite rifle, Annie Oakley could hit a playing card with the thin edge toward her or shatter a cigarette held in her husband's lips. Born into dire poverty, this young woman of the Wild West became the stuff of legend, a sharpshooter and performer who managed to see the world, meet royalty, and thrill crowds of thousands during her extraordinary career.

Originally named Phoebe Anne Moses, Annie was born into a large family of Quakers who had moved from western Pennsylvania into the new Midwestern frontier in 1856. Times were tough for the family of six children, especially after Annie's father died of exposure to the cold during a winter snowstorm when she was nine.

Because her mother was a district nurse and unable to care for her children while she traveled, the family was split up. Annie was sent to an orphanage. From there she was assigned to a farm family as a servant girl, where she was beaten and abused until she ran away. She managed to find her mother, by then remarried and living on a farm.

The next years were the happiest in Annie's childhood. Fearless and spirited, she rode horses and played in the woods of Darke County, Ohio. When she found her father's old rifle, she discovered a natural skill—sharpshooting. Her steady hand, dead-sharp eye, and instinctive timing made her a phenomenal hunter. In fact, she was able to hunt so successfully that she paid off the mortgage on her family farm by selling her kill in the town market.

As her fame grew, so did her challenges. After five years of illustrious hunting and marksmanship, she was asked to shoot a 207 match against the famed Frank Butler, a vaudeville performer. She defeated him by one point, but he fell in love with her anyway. They were later married.

Together, they became a world-renowned team. Frank not only taught his younger wife to read and write, but allowed her to take center stage during their act. With a girlish charm offsetting her astounding marksmanship, Annie thrilled crowds. In 1885 Butler left the act to manage his wife's career, and later was able to get her hired by the Buffalo Bill Wild West Show. She would remain with the show for over sixteen years.

Wearing fringed skirts, embroidered blouses, and a wide felt hat, this five-foot-tall, one hundred-pound woman was nicknamed "Little Sure Shot" by another performer, famed Indian leader

Sitting Bull. Her act was indeed impressive: she could flip a playing card into the air and perforate it with bullets as it fell or stand on a galloping horse and shoot the flames from a revolving wheel of candles.

In 1887, the Wild West Show traveled to Europe, where they performed for Queen Victoria of England and the Crown Prince of Germany.

Offstage, Annie was soft-spoken, very feminine, and led a quiet private life that never included the use of guns. Her favorite pastime was embroidery, and although she and Frank remained childless, she supported some eighteen orphan girls with the proceeds from her lucrative career.

Her career lasted her whole life, interrupted only by an injury from a train accident in 1901 that left her partially paralyzed. She recovered, acted in a few stage plays as Western heroines, then turned to demonstrations of her marksmanship for smaller groups. After a car accident in 1922, she was bedridden for the next four years. She died at the age of sixty-six and Frank died three weeks later.

SANDRA DAY O'CONNOR

SUPREME COURT JUSTICE

BORN *El Paso, Texas, March 26, 1930*

The appointment of the politically and judicially conservative Sandra Day O'Connor as the first woman Supreme Court Justice marked a turning point in our history. Having been for two decades more liberal and activist, the Court is now questioning its role in American affairs. Sandra's belief in the principle of judicial restraint, in which the Court bases its decisions on a strict reading of the Constitution and does not involve itself in lawmaking, has made her role a pivotal one on such issues as abortion, states' rights, and the rights of criminals.

Already reading and writing by the time she left kindergarten, Sandra was so smart that her parents sent her away from her hometown of Duncan to study at better schools in the city of El Paso. Living in the big city was quite a bit different from the days Sandra spent rounding up cattle and horseback riding on the Days' 170,000-acre ranch during her vacations.

When she was thirteen, Sandra grew too homesick to stay with her grandmother in El Paso and returned to live in Duncan for a year. But commuting to a school nearly twenty-five miles from home became too much for her, and she returned to El Paso where she later graduated from Austin High School at age sixteen.

Tall, pretty, and with a keen mind, Sandra entered Stanford University in Palo Alto, California, in 1946. It was rare for a woman to decide on a career in the law in those days. But after majoring in economics she applied and was accepted to Stanford Law School, where she excelled, graduating third in her class in 1952.

In addition to learning the intricacies of the law at Stanford, Sandra met two fellow classmates who would play major roles in her life. One of them was William Rehnquist, now the Chief Justice of the Supreme Court, who later helped President Ronald Reagan choose Sandra as his nominee for Supreme Court Justice in 1981.

The other man was John Jay O'Connor III, whom Sandra met in her senior year. They fell in love while working together on the prestigious journal the Stanford *Law Review*, and married in 1952, after Sandra graduated and before John began his last year in law school. Together they would have three sons and two exciting careers.

For Sandra, the first few years were professionally difficult. No major law firms would hire a woman attorney, and although Sandra would have preferred a private practice, she worked first for the San Mateo district attorney's office. The rest of her career would focus on public service in government offices.

Carefully balancing family life with their careers, the O'Connors became active in Republican politics and legal issues. In Phoenix, where they settled after John finished a stint in the Army, Sandra was in private practice from 1959 to 1965 and worked in a number of volunteer positions. She then made her way up the ranks of Arizona politics, from assistant attorney general to state senator.

It was as a tough but fair Arizona State Court of Appeals judge that Sandra drew the attention of her old classmate William Rehnquist and the new President, Ronald Reagan, in 1981. While campaigning, President Reagan had promised that if a position on the Court became available, he would make every effort to nominate a qualified woman to the position. Rehnquist, remembering the extremely capable young woman he'd known at Stanford, suggested Sandra Day O'Connor to the President when Justice Potter Stewart retired in 1981.

After lengthy congressional hearings that examined her views on political and judicial affairs, Sandra was confirmed as a Justice on September 21, 1981, a position she will hold for as long as she wishes to serve. Her intelligence and integrity, as well as her ground-breaking appointment to the high court, should remain an inspiration to all American women.

211

EUGENE O'NEILL

PLAYWRIGHT

BORN *New York, New York, October 16, 1888*
DIED *Boston, Massachusetts, November 27, 1953*

Eugene O'Neill, a troubled man who led a difficult life, wrote some of the most moving plays in American theater and is considered the father of modern American drama.

Eugene was born in a Broadway hotel and spent his youth around the theater. His father, James O'Neill, was a famous actor who took his wife and son with him on tours throughout the United States. When not with his parents, Eugene was in boarding school until he entered Princeton University at the age of eighteen. A year later, he was expelled for drunkenness and bad behavior, the first of many times that alcohol disrupted his life.

After leaving Princeton, he embarked upon rather unlikely careers—prospecting for gold in Central America and sailing the Atlantic on a steamship off and on for nearly three years and working as a reporter. After moving back to the States, he settled in New York City and lived in run-down waterfront rooming houses, taking on odd jobs while continuing to drink. In 1912, Eugene suffered a bout of tuberculosis and was hospitalized in a sanitarium.

It was during this year of convalescence that he decided to write plays. After his release he enrolled at Harvard University in Boston and studied playwriting for a year, moved back to New York, then went on to Provincetown, Massachusetts to join a recently organized theater group, the Provincetown Players. His first play, the one-act *Bound East for Cardiff,* opened there in 1916. When it was produced in New York, at the Playwright's Theater, it was critically acclaimed. Four years later, a full-length play, *Beyond the Horizon,* opened and won the first of four Pulitzer Prizes for Eugene. He would write over seventy plays in his lifetime, many of which were produced to commercial and critical acclaim. Eugene also won the Nobel Prize for Literature in 1936, the first American playwright ever to do so.

Despite this success, and the wealth and fame that resulted from it, Eugene led a troubled life. Married three times, and with three children, he was at best a neglectful husband and father. He drank far more than was good for his health, and yet he was completely self-absorbed with his physical well-being, almost becoming a hypochondriac in his middle years. He was tortured by his ambivalent feelings toward his parents—they had been dynamic, intense people, but neglectful of their only son. He spent much of his adult life searching for the protection and love he had missed in his youth.

It was probably from this inner torment that the genius in him sprung. The themes and images in his plays are echoes of the life he lived. Eugene O'Neill's work was autobiographical, and the emotional reality he expressed in his plays rang with the truth of lived experience. He wrote of the common man who, through some inner struggle, failed in life—men like those he'd met while living on the waterfront in New York City. He wrote of marriages destroyed by infidelity and bitterness, and of families lost in their own overwhelming loneliness and despair. All of his work focused on failed dreams—on the gulf between what one hopes for and what one finally achieves in an often unfair world.

Eugene spent almost all of the last thirty years of his life living in seclusion with his third wife, Carlotta. Despite critical acclaim, winning the Nobel Prize in 1936 and two Pulitzer Prizes in 1941 and 1943, his seclusion damaged his popularity with the theater-going public. In the later part of his life, he suffered from a rare brain disease which left him paralyzed and unable to write. He died in 1953.

Today his plays, like *Mourning Becomes Electra, Strange Interlude,* and *Long Day's Journey into Night,* are once again produced with some regularity and success. As Eugene had predicted in 1942, "There will again be an audience able to feel the inner meaning of plays dealing with the everlasting mystery and irony and tragedy of men's lives and dreams . . ."

214

J. ROBERT OPPENHEIMER

PHYSICIST

BORN *New York, New York, April 22, 1904*

DIED *Princeton, New Jersey, February 18, 1967*

When J. Robert Oppenheimer died in 1967, the world he left behind was far different from the one to which he was born at the beginning of this century. From the automobile and airplane to the telephone and television, technology had in all ways changed our lives.

Perhaps more than any other single invention, however, it is the atomic bomb and the total destruction it represents that most disturbs our lives. J. Robert Oppenheimer, considered "the father of the atomic bomb" in America, spent much of his life questioning his own responsibility to his country and to himself.

Born into a wealthy family, Robert grew up in New York City. He acquired an early love for mathematics and science and was very much a bookworm throughout his childhood, learning Greek, Latin, French, and German by the time he left high school. Awkward at most athletics, he became an accomplished sailor, a hobby he would enjoy throughout his life.

When he entered Harvard University in 1922, Robert's imagination truly flowered. He overloaded himself with courses in both science and the humanities. He graduated in just three years, then went on to study atomic energy and quantum mechanics in England and Germany.

Atomic energy and quantum mechanics were two relatively new scientific disciplines. At a very basic level, they are concerned with the way tiny particles of matter—atoms and their subparticles which include electrons, protons and neutrons—interact to create energy and heat. After receiving his Ph.D. in quantum mechanics in 1927 and another postdoctoral degree in 1928, Robert began teaching at the University of California at Berkeley and the California Institute of Technology in 1929.

216   As a teacher, he was affectionately known as "Oppie" to his students. His enthusiasm and intellectual generosity made him a very popular professor. At the same time, his political opinions were beginning to mature. As he experienced the United States in the midst of the Great Depression and heard stories of Jews being tortured in Germany in the 1930s, he, like many of his friends and associates, looked for answers to these problems by reading about and attending meetings that explored socialism and communism. Although he never joined the Communist Party, these earlier associations would haunt him later in his career.

In 1942, he was asked by President Roosevelt to head the U.S. research project to develop the atomic bomb, which would use energy released by splitting atoms to create a huge explosion. The United States, just entering World War II, felt an urgency to develop this weapon before its enemies, Germany and Japan, or its then ally, the Soviet Union, did. Robert and others recommended that a group of scientists be brought to a complex in the desert at Los Alamos, New Mexico, where their research could be conducted in complete secrecy.

Robert's research provided the focus for thousands of research scientists who worked tirelessly for two years until the first atomic bomb test explosion took place on July 16, 1945. Three weeks later, on August 6 and 9, President Truman ordered the bomb to be dropped on the Japanese cities of Hiroshima and Nagasaki, killing nearly 150,000 people and forcing Japan to surrender.

His work at Los Alamos completed, Robert returned to academia, becoming director of the new Institute for Advanced Study at Princeton. From there, he helped to formulate government policy on the use of atomic weapons, serving as chairman of the General Advisory to the Atomic Energy Commission from 1946 to 1952.

In late 1949, Robert was asked to head another research team, this one to explore the development of the far more powerful hydrogen bomb. Robert declined, citing his growing opposition to the use of nuclear weapons in general and the hydrogen bomb in particular.

In 1953, Robert became the target of a security investigation encouraged by Senator Joseph McCarthy, an anti-Communist zealot. Robert was accused of harboring Communist sympathies stemming from his early teaching days, and of being disloyal for not more forcefully supporting the hydrogen bomb. He was declared a security risk and stripped of the top-secret clearance required for much of his work.

Although he was later cleared of the most serious charges, the accusations cast a dark shadow on the rest of Robert's life. As director of the Institute for Advanced Study, he continued his pioneering work in physics and devoted much time to writing books that questioned the scientist's relationship to society and politics. In 1963 he was awarded the Atomic Energy Commission's highest award by President Lyndon Johnson, symbolically ending his public disgrace. He died in 1967.

ROBERT PEARY

EXPLORER

BORN *Cresson, Pennsylvania, May 6, 1856*
DIED *Washington, D.C., February 20, 1920*

According to his own published records, on the morning of April 6, 1909, the American explorer Robert Peary became the first man to reach the North Pole. While controversy rages today as to whether this determined man actually made it to the Pole or if he, in fact, falsified his own logs, there is no doubt that Robert Peary was one of America's most famous explorers. After nearly twenty-three years exploring the Arctic, he and a brave crew journeyed through blizzards and ice floes, dense fogs and survived bouts of frostbite, and navigated across nearly 1,000 miles of frozen land in that one expedition alone.

It is hard to imagine the kind of determination and energy required to make such a journey. Indeed, Robert Peary, the son of a lumber manufacturer, was at once insecure about his abilities and yet determined to make his mark in history. This inner conflict infused him with the energy he needed to face immense physical hardships and the loneliness that comes from months isolated in a frozen landscape. It may also have caused him to lay claim to a discovery he, in fact, did not make.

It was not until Robert was nearly thirty that the lure of the North beckoned him. He had attended Bowdoin College from 1873 to 1877, where he was a bright, intuitive student of science and mathematics, and later he became a civil engineer with the U.S. Navy. After serving on an expedition to survey a canal route across Nicaragua in 1884, Robert read an account of the exploration of Greenland by a Norwegian explorer that rekindled an interest in the Arctic. "The 'arctic fever' . . . entered my veins then, and I came to have a feeling of fatality, a feeling that the reason and intent of my existence was the solution of the mystery of the frozen vastness of the Arctic."

220   His first trip was a short expedition accompanied only by a Danish guide. Later he would take an eighteen-month leave to explore, with his wife Josephine Diebitsch and a seven-member crew, much of Greenland's interior. By the time he returned from that expedition, during which he suffered a broken leg, he had established an international reputation. Able now to raise money for his expeditions, he and financier Norris Jessup formed the Peary Arctic Club to finance his future journeys north.

With each expedition, Robert was able to add more information about this largely unexplored territory. He revised maps of the area, made an in-depth study of Eskimo life, and even found meteorites weighing from 90 to 100 tons, two of which, incredibly, he brought back with him.

But it is that final expedition, the one that made his place in history secure, for which we remember him best. Five brave and able men, including Matthew Henson, a black American who served as Peary's personal aide during all but his first trip, and four Eskimos accompanied him on the last part of this treacherous journey. With the help of thirty-eight stalwart Eskimo dogs to pull the sledges, Robert and his men traveled through ice, snow, and unbearable cold.

On that bright April morning, the crew arrived at what they believed to be the North Pole. In his journal Robert described the moment like this: "East, west and north had disappeared for us. One direction remained and that was south. Every breeze which could possibly blow upon us, no matter from what point on the horizon, must be a south wind. Where we were, one day and one night constituted a year, a hundred such days and nights constituted a century."

Despite the continuing challenge to his discovery, starting with one made by Frederick Cook, who claimed to have reached the North Pole a year before him, Robert's last years were spent as a national hero. He received the French Legion of Honor and served as president of the American Geographical Society in 1903. He died in 1920.

MAXWELL EVARTS PERKINS

EDITOR

BORN *New York, New York, September 20, 1884*
DIED *Stamford, Connecticut, June 17, 1947*

"There could be nothing so important as a book could be," Max Perkins, the dean of American editors, once said. Almost singlehandedly, he championed a twentieth-century explosion of American writers, introducing such illustrious authors as Ernest Hemingway, F. Scott Fitzgerald, and, most notably, Thomas Wolfe to an eager public.

The son of a lawyer and grandson of a U.S. senator and former Secretary of State, William Maxwell Evarts Perkins grew up in a privileged atmosphere in New York City. A good student, he attended the prestigious St. Paul's School in Concord, New Hampshire, then went on to study at Harvard. Despite the fact that Max always had been a rather slow, even unenthusiastic reader, a relationship with an inspiring English professor changed him profoundly. Perkins fell in love with literature and language.

After graduating in 1907, Max went to work for the *New York Times* newspaper in Manhattan. Covering the police beat during late-night hours, Max volunteered for many risky assignments. Despite the exciting nature of his work, Max soon grew weary of the daily newspaper grind. While courting the woman he would marry in 1910, Max considered the responsibilities of a family, and decided to leave the newspaper world behind.

Max then took a job in the advertising department at the book publisher Charles Scribner's Sons. He joined the company in 1910, stayed in the advertising department for four years, and then was hired as an assistant in the editorial department. He would work there in various capacities until he was appointed editor-in-chief and vice president, a position he held for twenty years.

223

In 1914, when Max first began his work as an editor, Scribner's was an old-fashioned publishing company, with a roster of authors rooted in an eighteenth-century literary style. Max, on the other hand, felt that the company should assume a prominent role in the modern publishing world. He began to urge older, more conservative senior members of the firm to consider younger, preferably American, authors.

His first "discovery" was F. Scott Fitzgerald, a young Midwestern writer who wrote of the American "jazz age" in the 1920s. Ernest Hemingway, too, was largely unknown when Max decided to publish his innovative short stories and novels. A devoted editor, friend, and confidant, Max was able to keep authors working when their enthusiasm and energy lagged. He even advanced them money and helped arbitrate unhappy romances when necessary. Most importantly he also insisted that any editorial changes be made according to the writer's own ideas.

Perhaps his most famous relationship was that with Thomas Wolfe. Insecure but ambitious, Wolfe had created a massive semiautobiographical novel that had taken years to write. But the manuscript required substantial changes to make it publishable. Using all of his instincts and knowledge, Max was able to gently guide Wolfe through a meticulous revision. The result was the masterpiece *Look Homeward, Angel.*

Suffering from a number of respiratory infections, Max's final years were painful. His last two projects, however, proved his talent for seeing the future of literature. As he was being taken to the hospital for the last time, he made certain that his daughter would deliver the ground-breaking manuscripts, *Cry, the Beloved Country* by South African author Alan Paton and the World War II masterpiece *From Here to Eternity* by James Jones, to his office.

Confident of his own talent and that of his authors, Max Perkins always felt that "a writer's best work comes entirely from himself. . . . An editor does not add to a book. At best he serves as a handmaiden to an author." His enormous success and high professional regard is testament to this credo.

224

MATTHEW CALBRAITH PERRY

NAVAL LEADER

B O R N *Newport, Rhode Island, April 10, 1794*

D I E D *New York, New York, March 4, 1858*

In Newport, Rhode Island, a statue commemorates the outstanding accomplishments of Commander Matthew Perry. Across
the globe, in Kurihama, Japan, another monument is dedicated to
the same man. Responsible for establishing relations between Japan and the United States as well as overseeing the modernization
of the American Navy, this man was one of America's first true
naval heroes.

Born in Newport in the late 1700s, Matthew grew up near
the sea, and witnessed both the age of the great whaling ships and

the birth of American naval forces. The lure of the sea must have been quite strong, for not only did Matthew enter the young American navy before he reached the age of fifteen, but his older brother, Oliver—also a naval hero—did too.

Matthew's first tour of duty had him serving on Oliver's ship for over a year, then transferring to the *President*, commanded by a tough disciplinarian named John Rodgers, under whom he would serve during the War of 1812. Matthew himself would later be known for his almost haughty attitude toward his men and colleagues.

After being promoted to lieutenant, Matthew was transferred to another ship, which was forced out of action and harbored in New London, Connecticut. There, while waiting to be reassigned, he met and later married Jane Slidell of New York, with whom he would have ten children.

His next assignments took him around the globe. Matthew was put in charge of a program to transport freed African slaves to Liberia. He was later assigned to transport an American diplomat, John Randolph, to Russia. Matthew's own diplomatic skills, combined with a rather austere but definite charm, brought him to the attention of the Czar, who invited him to join the Russian naval service.

As flattering as such an offer was, he returned to the United States, where he was later appointed Captain of the New York naval yard, one of the largest yards in the country.

For over ten years, Matthew undertook an intense overhauling and expansion of the U.S. naval system. He had a profound belief in the importance of a strong, well-trained navy, and under his administration a dramatic modernization of the U.S. Navy took place. He helped persuade the Navy Department to build a series of new steam-driven warships and institute a weapons testing program. He oversaw the creation of a museum of naval history, the publication *Naval Magazine,* and the preparation of the first course of instruction at the Naval Academy at Annapolis.

But his greatest moment came in 1852 when selected by the Navy Department to undertake what was at that time the most important and delicate mission ever entrusted to an American Naval officer—the negotiation of a trade agreement with Japan, a nation that had long since closed its ports to any outside influence.

Armed with four warships and a letter from President Fillmore to the Emperor of Japan, Matthew set sail for the Far East. Matthew arrived in Edo (then the name of Tokyo, the capital of Japan) and eight months later his real work began. Shrouding himself in mystery and issuing veiled threats of military might to minor Japanese government officials, he finessed his way into a meeting with the high princes of the secluded Emperor.

America wanted to trade with Japan and take advantage of its strategic position in the rich Asia-Pacific region. Understanding not only the military but also the political importance of his mission, Matthew was able to persuade the Japanese to accede to American desires the following year.

227

His last long journey home from Japan caused a serious decline in Matthew's health. Unable to take command of another mission, he instead worked quietly on a report of his expedition to Japan. He managed to finish the three-volume tome by the time he died in 1858, chronicling the greatest adventure of his life.

MOLLY PITCHER (MARY LUDWIG HAYS McCAULEY)

NURSE, LAUNDRESS, SOLDIER

BORN *Trenton, New Jersey, October 13, 1754*

DIED *Carlisle, Pennsylvania, January 22, 1832*

"**M**olly Pitcher," one of the most colorful legends of the American Revolutionary War, was perhaps the first American woman to take part in a military battle, and she performed with legendary distinction.

Little is known about the life of Molly Pitcher before the war. Her real name was Mary Ludwig and her father was one of the many early German immigrants to settle in New Jersey.

Like many young women of the time, Molly first made her living as a servant. While working for Dr. William Irvine, she met and fell in love with John Hays, a barber. They were married when she was not yet fifteen and eventually had one son. Molly and her family lived a quiet life in the rural Pennsylvania village of Carlisle.

Everything changed for Mary and her husband with the start of the American Revolution. John joined the Continental Army as an artillery officer. Molly followed him to war, to wash his clothes and cook for him—a common practice at the time. Described as highly excitable and rather talkative, the plucky Molly served right alongside her husband for three years, enduring all the hardships and dangers of army life.

In June 1778, George Washington's forces fought a major battle against the British at Monmouth, New Jersey. It was a broiling day, supposedly 96 degrees in the shade, and Molly and the other wives worked hard to haul water to men fighting in the front lines. Carrying the water in buckets or pitchers, Molly was given the nickname "Molly Pitcher."

Suddenly, during one British charge, Molly saw her husband fall—either shot or overcome by the heat. He had to be carried from the field, and it looked as if no one could work his important cannon. But the enraged Molly took his place. Swearing vengeance on the British, she grabbed the ramrod used to shove cannonballs down into the cannon, and continued to work the gun for the rest of the battle.

After this display of independence, Molly Pitcher became a legend almost overnight. General Washington personally congratulated her on her bravery the next day, and she was showered with gifts by the allied French officers. She was made a sergeant, and officially served nearly eight years in the army.

Unfortunately for Molly, her service soon became rather routine once again. Her husband recovered and until his death in 1789, she lived with him in the army's barracks at Carlisle, her hometown. There she was employed in such traditional women's roles as cook and laundress for the soldiers. Described as both strict and tender, she cared not only for her own son but for the children of other military families.

After her husband's death, she had enough money to run a general store. Later, she entered into a bad marriage to Sergeant George McCauley, who was said to have lived off her earnings and beaten her. When he left her penniless, it seemed as if she would live her final years in poverty and obscurity. Instead, the state of Pennsylvania voted her a generous pension and again commended her for the heroism she had displayed on the field of battle. She died in 1832.

POCAHONTAS

INDIAN PRINCESS

BORN *Richmond, Virginia, 1595 or 1596*

DIED *Gravesend, England, March 21, 1617*

Surrounded by legend and myth, the life of Pocahontas intrigues both professional and amateur historians to this day. Indian princess, savior of the white man, Christian wife of a British subject, Pocahontas did indeed lead a colorful life.

What we know of her childhood is generally based on speculation. The favorite daughter of the powerful Powhatan, chief of a confederation of Algonquin tribes, Pocahontas (meaning "playful one") was probably a high-spirited young girl, raised with all the privileges accorded an Indian princess.

One April day in 1607, when Pocahontas was just a youngster, perhaps eleven or twelve, a white man, Captain John Smith, an explorer and settler of the new Virginia colony called Jamestown, entered her sheltered life. On a scouting mission, he was separated from his party and captured by Powhatan's men.

According to Smith, the only eyewitness to publicize his experience, he was kept prisoner and fed well for weeks, then taken to see the chief, Powhatan. When Powhatan ordered Smith killed, feisty Pocahontas rushed toward the captive and cradled his head in her arms, pleading that her father not kill the white man. Smith was released and sent back to Jamestown, where soon everyone knew about the brave Indian princess named Pocahontas.

The next several winters were hard on the ill-prepared Jamestown settlers. According to some historical sources, if Pocahontas herself hadn't brought huge amounts of food to feed all the settlers, many would have died and the settlement most certainly would have failed.

In the spring of 1613, while visiting a local Indian chief, Pocahontas was kidnapped by an English captain. Hoping to use Powhatan's beautiful daughter as leverage against further Indian attacks, the English took her to Jamestown and then to another nearby settlement. A period of relative peace ensued, due as much to the growing strength of the settlement as the princess's presence in the camp.

Pocahontas, who had little or no formal education, was treated well by her captives. She was taught English and given instruction in Christianity, to which she converted. A year later, she met and married John Rolfe, a prosperous British businessman, with whom she had a son.

Invited to England, the Rolfe family was treated like royalty. Pocahontas, presented to Queen Anne, was the toast of a whirlwind social season. But as the year wore on, Pocahontas became quite ill and, just as the Rolfes set sail for America, she died. She was buried at Gravesend, England.

For eight years, peace between the Indians and the white man was maintained. Just a few years after Pocahontas's death, however, the battle lines were once again drawn. As a symbol of peace, Pocahontas endured. But her image also frustrated many British, who believed that all Indians, if given the chance, would welcome the white man's customs and idea of civilization. Many Indians would die to prove that theory wrong and protect their own rich and vital culture.

EDGAR ALLAN POE

WRITER

BORN *Boston, Massachusetts, January 19, 1809*

DIED *Baltimore, Maryland, October 7, 1849*

Deep human emotions—the desperate heartache of unre-quited love, the breathtaking terror of murder, the backbreaking weight of guilt—are evoked with such precision and feeling in the poetry and prose of Edgar Allan Poe that critics and readers continue to be intrigued with his work nearly 140 years after his death. The author of lyrical poetry like "Annabel Lee" and "The Raven" was also America's first craftsman of horror and mystery writing. "The Fall of the House of Usher" and "The Tell-Tale Heart" are just two of the spine-tingling tales for which Poe has become famous.

His own life was an extremely troubled one. Drunkenness and perhaps drug addiction are two vices attributed to Poe; womanizing is another. The extent to which he was afflicted is debated, but it is certain that Edgar lacked the capacity to deal with everyday life in a practical way. Instead, his brilliant imagination fatally combined with an inner torment to create in him not only a genius for writing, but also a prescription for personal doom.

Edgar was orphaned when he was only two years old, and never knew his parents. While his brother was taken in by paternal grandparents and his sister by close friends, Edgar became part of a prominent Richmond, Virginia, family. John Allan, a merchant, and his wife Frances were unable to have children of their own. Frances especially was thrilled to take Edgar in.

But the relationship between Edgar and his stepfather was fraught with problems. Marital difficulties would strain the Allan household, with Edgar constantly siding with Frances against her husband. In addition, Edgar's creative, impulsive character grated against John's strict nature.

Edgar was an extremely bright young man. He did well in his studies at the University of Virginia—until he was expelled for failing to pay his losses at cards. After a series of arguments, and after Frances' death, John remarried and disowned Edgar, leaving him destitute. He wrote poetry and short stories constantly, most of which would later become American classics, but had trouble getting them published. He never could seem to make enough money to keep a roof over his head and food on the table. When he married his young cousin, Virginia Clemm, his responsibilities, and worries over fulfilling them, mounted, especially because his wife would spend her whole life suffering from tuberculosis.

Edgar, Virginia, and Virginia's mother went from city to city as Edgar took one job after another at various prestigious literary

235

journals. While his work was published more and more, he also became a well-respected and rather famous critic and editor.

But Edgar had a dark side, a side that drank too much and stayed away from home for days at a time. His melancholy sprees cost him every job he ever had, and kept him from fulfilling his dream of starting his own magazine. Instead, his life was spent deep in poverty and despair, always on the brink of disaster.

And yet it seems that his life experiences might have inspired him to create the mesmerizing stories and poems during his forty difficult years. All of the emotions he felt about his life—despair at the loss of his natural parents, anger at his foster father for leaving him penniless, sadness over his wife's illness, disappointment in his own failings—fueled in him the passion to write the lyrics of heartache and the eerie tales of murder and betrayal for which we admire him.

Edgar died in Baltimore after a five-day drinking binge. Rescued drugged and drunk from a tavern by an old friend, he was nursed for days in a nearby hospital before he died, of complications due to alcoholism. Today Poe is recognized throughout the world as a master storyteller and poet.

E L V I S
P R E S L E Y

R O C K   A N D   R O L L   S I N G E R

B O R N *Tupelo, Mississippi, January 8, 1935*

D I E D *Memphis, Tennessee, August 16, 1977*

"They get set off by shock waves of hysteria, going into frenzies of screeching and wailing, winding up in tears." So *Life* magazine described the reactions of Elvis Presley's fans. One of the most important influences on modern popular music, Elvis Presley was a sensation throughout his career of more than twenty years, and he has become a legend since his death in 1977.

His meteoric rise to stardom masked a difficult childhood. His father, Vernon, served nine months in prison for forgery when Elvis was just three years old, and in 1948 the Presley family moved to Memphis after Vernon was accused of selling bootleg whiskey. The Presleys were always on the edge of poverty and Vernon drifted from one job to another.

The Presleys were a religious family, and it was in church that Elvis began to sing, first in choir and later at revival meetings in the community. While still in elementary school, he entered an amateur singing contest sponsored by the radio station WELO in which he won fifth prize.

Elvis taught himself to play the guitar immediately after his mother gave him one for his eleventh birthday. Never able to read music, he instead learned hillbilly tunes and black blues songs by listening to records. Elvis developed his talent naturally from many different kinds of music, but was never sure he wanted to sing for a living.

During the summer after his high school graduation, Elvis stopped in at the Memphis Recording Service in Memphis to make a record for his mother, Gladys. He paid four dollars to make recordings of two songs, "My Happiness" and "That's When Your Heartaches Begin." When Sam Phillips, the president of the company, heard them, he signed Elvis to a contract with Sun Records, launching one of the biggest careers in musical history.

238

Elvis was an overnight sensation. His music was first played over Memphis radio and within weeks his reputation spread throughout the South. Colonel Tom Parker, a music agent, took Elvis under his wing, sending him on the first of many concert tours. Within a year, the RCA Victor Record Company bought Elvis's contract from Sun Records, recording and releasing five Elvis Presley albums simultaneously. Each would sell over a million copies within a year. Elvis's earthy energy epitomized rock and roll, influencing future rockers from the Beatles to Bruce Springsteen.

His personal appearances drew screams of delight from female fans and his masculinity earned the envy of teenaged males. But while teenagers adored him, their parents frequently did not. His stage mannerisms, described by one reporter as resembling "a striptease with clothes on," included gyrating hips, suggestive facial expressions, and a defiant stance. By today's standards, Elvis's performances were mild, but to the parents and critics of the 1950s, they represented a revolution. And the youth of the 1950s and 1960s joined that revolution by the millions.

At the same time that his musical career was skyrocketing, Elvis was signed to a Hollywood movie contract. He went on to make thirty-one movies and two documentaries, including *Jailhouse Rock*, *Love Me Tender*, and *Girls, Girls, Girls*.

By all accounts, Elvis was generous to a fault with his family and friends. He spent the enormous fortune he amassed on extravagant gifts—like Cadillacs and mink coats—sometimes giving them to mere acquaintances. He was married for over twelve years to Priscilla Presley, with whom he had a daughter, Lisa Marie.

The remarkable contributions Elvis made to music and to the spirit of America during his lifetime persist today. Although the later part of his life was marred by illness and a devastating addiction to prescription drugs, his millions of fans still remember him as the "King of Rock and Roll."

239

JACKIE ROBINSON

BASEBALL PLAYER

BORN *Cairo, Georgia, January 31, 1919*

DIED *Stamford, Connecticut, October 24, 1972*

On April 15, 1947, a momentous event in sports history occurred. Jackie Robinson, the first black ever to play in baseball's major leagues, strode onto Ebbets Field in Brooklyn, New York. Wearing Dodgers' uniform number 42, Jackie took his place at bat, forever changing the face of professional athletics in the United States.

Before Jackie Robinson arrived on the scene, baseball was segregated—blacks ` played in the Negro leagues while whites played in the majors. Branch Rickey, general manager of the

Dodgers from 1942 to 1950, realized that both leagues were suffering from the effects of segregation and decided to remedy the
situation by signing a black player to his team. He knew that
whoever became the first black player would need courage and
strength to meet the challenge of racism and ignorance in his
teammates, competitors and audience.

In Jackie, Branch found all that and more. Jack Roosevelt
Robinson, born in Georgia and raised in California, had seen his
share of prejudice. He fought against this injustice every step of
the way. As a child he battled with white neighbors who tried to
run the Robinson family off the block; in the Army he took on his
superiors to see that he and his fellow black soldiers were given
the promotions and salary increases they were due. His toughness
and determination, as well as his phenomenal athletic ability,
attracted the admiration of many and, finally, the attention of
Branch Rickey.

When the Dodgers first approached Jackie, he was playing
for the Kansas City Monarchs in the Negro American Baseball
League. His talents had been obvious since he was a preschooler,
when he could hit the ball harder and run faster than kids nine
and ten years old. And he only improved with age. At the University of California at Los Angeles (UCLA), where he majored in
physical education, he was UCLA's first black four-letter man,
excelling in basketball, football, and track and field. If he'd been
white, he would have been signed to a major league team immediately, but he was relegated to the Negro leagues until after World
War II.

The reaction to Branch Rickey's courageous decision was
decidedly mixed—some fans and players were outraged and reacted with violence; others were grateful that a fundamental barrier to equality had been crossed.

It was Jackie Robinson's personality that made the difference. Faced with racial slurs from his opponents, even from his

241

teammates, Jackie held his ground, never giving in to anger but instead proving his ability in game after game. In an interview with a reporter, he described how he felt about this enormous challenge, "These days keep reminding me of something my mother told me when I was a little kid. She told me that the words they say about you can't hurt you. And when they see that, they'll quit saying them."

Despite the added pressures he faced, Jackie quickly proved himself to be one of the finest players, black or white, in baseball history. After his first season, he was named Rookie of the Year. In 1949 he was named the Most Valuable Player of the National League. He averaged over 100 runs scored in each of the ten seasons he played with the Dodgers, and led the team to six World Series. He retired from baseball in 1956 with a lifetime batting average of .311. In 1962, he was the first black to be elected to baseball's Hall of Fame.

Jackie said himself that "A life is not important except in the impact it has on other lives." Today there are many black players in all professional sports, and some of them have gone on to become executives and television sportscasters. Without Jackie Robinson, and the dignity and respect he engendered in the American public, the struggle for equality in professional sports might have been far more violent and prolonged.

THE
ROCKEFELLER
FAMILY

At the center of twentieth-century international economics and industry, one American family has exerted more influence than any other. With holdings now estimated to be well over $1.5 billion, not including vast art collections and real estate holdings, the Rockefeller family remains one of the wealthiest dynastys in the world.

John D. Rockefeller was born in 1839 to a lower middle-class family near Richford, New York, where his father was a traveling salesman of patent medicines at country fairs. John D.

John D. Rockefeller and John D. Rockefeller, Jr.

would put his modest beginnings behind him, however, soon after he graduated from high school.

Spending a few years as a bookkeeper for a financial house in Cleveland, he then invested his savings in an oil refinery. In 1865, he brought his brother William into the firm and began what would become the largest corporation in the history of the United States, the Standard Oil Company of Ohio.

With blinding ambition that frequently crossed over to ruthlessness, John D. set about destroying his competition with his highly organized and already wealthy company. He bought out company after company, and expanded his own business to include pipeline facilities and financial institutions. By 1880, John D. controlled more than 95 percent of the oil industry and became the nation's first billionaire.

When he officially retired in 1911, his son, John D., Jr. (1874–1960), was already thirty-seven years old, and well versed in the family's business affairs. John D., Jr., would begin the Rockefellers' relationship to the banking industry by establishing the Chase Bank, since 1955 the Chase Manhattan, still one of the nation's largest international banking institutions.

At the same time, John D., Jr., would change the Rockefeller image dramatically, a process begun by his father. As well as increasing the family's wealth, he and his son John D. III would contribute millions of dollars to various universities, museums, parklands, and other public projects. Lincoln Center for the Performing Arts and Rockefeller Center, both in New York City, and the restoration of colonial Williamsburg, Virginia, are just three of the mammoth projects undertaken with Rockefeller money.

This sense of public mission was passed on to John D., Jr.'s five sons, known as the Rockefeller Brothers. They would diversify the family's influence even further, into politics and high-profile economic policy making. Nelson Rockefeller (1908–79) became governor of New York for four terms, then was appointed

Vice President of the United States under Gerald Ford. David (1915–) was the president, then chairman of Chase Manhattan Bank and private economic adviser to many heads of state, here and abroad. Winthrop Rockefeller (1910–) served two terms as governor of Arkansas, while Laurance (1906–) has concentrated on real estate and conservation. John D. III helped to establish the United Negro College Fund and has amassed one of the largest collections of Asian art in the world.

Today, although the Rockefeller wealth is still extraordinary, it is dispersed. From John D.'s one son to John D., Jr.'s six children have come ninety-seven direct heirs to the family fortune. While the Rockefeller name is still associated with economic and political power (John D. IV is a senator and former governor from West Virginia and David Jr. is taking an active role in his family's many philanthropies), the intense concentration of wealth no longer exists. Nevertheless, the influence of the Rockefeller family will continue to exert itself in financial and charitable circles and in the imaginations of millions of Americans.

ELEANOR ROOSEVELT

SOCIAL REFORMER, DIPLOMAT

BORN *New York, New York, October 11, 1884*
DIED *New York, New York, November 7, 1962*

The niece of one United States President and the wife of another, Eleanor Roosevelt might easily have been overshadowed by the men in her life. Instead, she carved out a remarkable career as a social reformer and diplomat.

Born Anna Eleanor to Elliot Roosevelt, the younger brother of President Theodore Roosevelt, and Anna Hall, Eleanor had a rather difficult childhood. She was a solemn, reserved child who never won her mother's affection. Her father, whom she adored, was an alcoholic, and although he loved his daughter, he was

Eleanor Roosevelt (center) at a reception in Washington, D.C.

undependable. Both parents died by the time Eleanor was twelve, and she was shunted off to live with her mother's family.

Eleanor's first chance to blossom came when she was sent to boarding school in London, at the age of fifteen. There she was introduced to some of the most compelling social and political issues of the day—racism, anti-Semitism, and the fight for independence of impoverished countries. She would remain dedicated to such causes throughout her life.

Back in New York City at the turn of the century, Eleanor found herself caught up in the debutante party life that accompanied the wealth and prestige of being a Roosevelt. But her new-found commitment to social reform was also kept. She was active in a number of organizations dedicated to helping the poor and disadvantaged, and joined the National Consumer League when she was just eighteen.

It was at this time that she became romantically involved with her distant cousin, Franklin Delano Roosevelt. Although she was quiet and aloof and he warm and spontaneous, the two fell in love. They were married in 1905 and in the years that followed set up households in New York City, Albany, and then Washington, depending on the turn in Franklin's career. While Eleanor bore him six children, one of whom died in infancy, Franklin first became a member of the New York State legislature, then assistant secretary of the Navy.

It wasn't until World War I in 1917 that Eleanor again became involved in social activity. She plunged in with characteristic zeal, coordinating Red Cross activities and speaking out at political rallies.

After the war Eleanor became active in the League of Women Voters, drafting laws to provide equal representation for men and women and helping promote other women's rights causes. When her husband was tragically stricken with paralyzing

247

polio in 1921, Eleanor had enough recognition and political know-how to take on many of his public commitments.

Although her marriage to Franklin grew strained, largely due to their very different personalities, they shared a commitment to the poor of America. Eleanor campaigned for Franklin, helping to elect him to a record four terms in the White House.

The United States was in the depths of the Great Depression during his first term. Millions of people were out of work. While Franklin put in motion the policies of the New Deal, which included widespread welfare policies, Eleanor visited relief centers across the country and became a champion of Appalachian farmers struggling to reclaim land they had lost.

Not content to merely speak out on issues, Eleanor led by example. She herself visited wounded veterans in Army hospitals around the world during and after World War II. She personally bore witness to the terrible conditions in the depressed coal mine regions of Pennsylvania and Kentucky. She championed the cause of civil rights for black Americans, helping to make possible the Fair Employment Practices Commission, which explored discrimination in the workplace. An accomplished author, she wrote a number of books and newspaper and magazine columns throughout her career.

Most important, by her very enthusiasm and determination, she set an example for a new generation of women in politics. Even after Franklin died in 1945, Eleanor continued to speak her mind and carry forward New Deal policies as one of the most effective women in politics.

When President Truman nominated her a delegate to the United Nations, her vision of peace and dignity for all mankind had a new forum. It was largely through her efforts that in 1948 the U.N. passed the Universal Declaration of Human Rights. Until her death at the age of seventy-eight, Eleanor remained a valiant champion of social reform.

248

GEORGE HERMAN "BABE" RUTH

ATHLETE

BORN *Baltimore, Maryland, February 6, 1895*

DIED *New York, New York, August 16, 1948*

George Herman Ruth, known as "the Babe" to his millions of fans, was one of America's greatest athletes, and certainly the most celebrated baseball player in the history of the sport. A gregarious, generous, and outspoken man, Babe Ruth won the hearts of millions of people around the world.

Babe Ruth never talked much about his childhood or his family. Many people thought he was an orphan, but Babe denied that rumor, telling a reporter, "My folks lived in Baltimore and my father worked in the [waterfront] district. We were very poor.

And there were times when we never knew where the next meal was coming from. But I never minded. I was no worse off than the other kids with whom I played and fought."

Babe discovered baseball when he was just seven years old. Sent to an institution for wayward children, St. Mary's Industrial School for Boys, Babe was taken under the wing of Brother Matthias, a member of the Catholic teaching staff at the school. Brother Matthias introduced the unruly youth to school athletics, most likely hoping to refocus some of Babe's considerable energy. It worked. "Once I had been introduced to school athletics," Ruth recalled in an interview with writer Paul Gallico, "I was satisfied and happy."

His determination and sheer love of the sport would change baseball forever. When he was nineteen, he was offered a contract with the Baltimore Orioles' minor league team by its owner, Jack Dunn. According to some sources, it was Babe's gentle disposition and youthful looks that prompted his teammates to nickname him Babe. Others report that it was the team's coach who gave him his famous moniker by remarking, on the day he reported to the Orioles' clubhouse for practice, "Well, here's Jack's newest babe now!" In any event, the nickname stuck.

Babe was signed as a pitcher, and pitch he did. During his first season, he played first for the Orioles, then for the Boston Red Sox and its farm team in Providence. While sources differ on the exact number of games Babe played, his record was outstanding. He won approximately 22 games and lost just 9.

Back in Boston with the Red Sox the next season, he helped them to win the World Series against the Brooklyn Dodgers. In 1918 they won the World Series against the Chicago Cubs, with Babe setting a World Series record of 29 consecutive scoreless innings, including a 14-inning game.

Although his pitching arm was extraordinary, Babe was also developing a reputation as a powerful left-handed batter. In 1919 he broke all previous major-league records by hitting 29 home runs in one season. In 1920 the New York Yankees bought his contract from the Red Sox for about $125,000 and a $300,000 loan to the Boston owner, a record sum of money at that time.

While he also played center field and first base, he was most famous for his seasons in right field. With the Yankees, he earned the American League's Most Valuable Player award in 1923, and, with Lou Gehrig, led the league in home runs in 1919–24 and 1926–31. In 1927, Ruth hit a record 60 home runs during the season. As a Yankee, he played in seven World Series and later, as a Boston Brave, he hit three home runs during one of his last professional games on May 25, 1935.

More than his incredible statistics, however, it is Babe's personality and his impact on the game of baseball that are remembered. He sparked a wider interest in baseball at home and abroad, raised the general level of player salaries, and became one of the first real sports stars of the twentieth century.

He loved to have fun, sometimes to his detriment. His drinking and carousing cost him professional and popular support. At one point, he was barred from playing for a short time for his antics. But he was also kind and sensitive, understanding the tremendous responsibility he had to his fans, especially the millions of kids who adored him.

251

Today, some of Ruth's records have been broken—Hank Aaron hit more home runs in his career, and Roger Maris hit more in one season than Babe Ruth ever did. But the fun and excitement he brought to the game would be hard to match. When he died of throat cancer, he left some of his considerable estate to the Babe Ruth Foundation, an organization he founded in 1947 to aid underprivileged children.

JONAS EDWARD SALK

IMMUNOLOGIST

BORN *New York, New York, October 28, 1914*

In the late 1940s and early 1950s, *poliomyelitis*, an infectious disease of the spinal cord, struck the United States in epidemic proportions. In 1952 alone 50,000 people, mostly children, were stricken and 3,300 victims died. Dr. Jonas Salk, already known as an expert on epidemics from his work on influenza viruses, was made director of a three-year project to investigate the polio virus by the National Foundation for Infantile Paralysis in 1949. A little over three years later, he announced that he and his staff had developed a successful vaccine against this dreaded disease.

Jonas Salk (center), watching as a young woman is vaccinated with his famous polio vaccine

Jonas was born to a lower-middle-class New York family in 1914. The oldest of three brothers, he was a very quiet child, small and thin, who was not a particularly gifted student or very popular with his classmates. Despite these factors, Jonas later reported that he knew even then that "someday I shall grow up and do something in my own way, without anyone telling me how."

Jonas dreamed of being a doctor—not to practice medicine, but to do research. He studied at City College for his Bachelor of Science, then received his M.D. at New York University School of Medicine. After serving a two-year internship at Mount Sinai Hospital, where he was remembered as "the most stable young man in the place" by the doctor in charge, Jonas was given a fellowship to the University of Michigan to study epidemiology, the science of investigating the origin of disease and how it spreads.

In epidemiology, Jonas found his niche. The study of disease —where it comes from, what causes it, and how to cure or prevent it—was still relatively young and Jonas found the challenge stimulating. He focused his research on viruses, the most complicated of disease-causing organisms, and undertook an investigation of influenza viruses until asked to join the fight against polio.

Jonas knew that the only way to stop the spread of the crippling disease was by injecting a vaccine—a serum that contains a small, mild amount of the killed virus, not enough to cause disease—into the body. The body would then use its own defense system—the immune system—to render the killed virus harmless. Once the immune system has done this, the body is protected against exposure to a live virus.

Working seven days a week, often twenty hours at a stretch, Jonas and his staff broke down the complicated structure of the polio virus and discovered a vaccine. Testing it on himself, his wife, and his children, he guaranteed its safety and effectiveness to the world in 1953. By the end of 1954, mass vaccinations of

253

schoolchildren began, with Jonas himself taking part in the process. Using considerable sensitivity and tenderness, Jonas would smile at children he treated until they smiled back. He'd never vaccinate a child crying at the sight of the needle; he gave his own children the shots while they slept.

In 1963 Jonas founded the Salk Institute for Biological Studies at La Jolla, California. A major part of his later work has been concerned with the development of a vaccine against cancer. Today scientists studying immunology and epidemiology have come a long way in understanding viruses and cancers, thanks in part to Jonas Salk's dedicated contributions.

ELIZABETH ANN BAYLEY SETON

RELIGIOUS LEADER

BORN *New York, New York, August 28, 1774*

DIED *Emmitsburg, Maryland, January 4, 1821*

Although Elizabeth Bayley Seton was born to a prominent Protestant family, she would grow up to become the first and only American Catholic saint. Her life story is one of selflessness and devotion to religious and moral ideals.

Elizabeth was only three years old when her mother died. Her father, Dr. Richard Bayley, and a stepmother would raise and educate her. Recognizing in his daughter an extraordinary intelligence, Dr. Bayley encouraged her to be independent and moral.

When she was nineteen years old, and considered one of

New York City's most beautiful debutantes, she married a wealthy young merchant named William Magee Seton. Over the next eight years they would have five children together, two boys and three girls.

As much as she loved her family, however, Elizabeth's true passion lay in helping the less fortunate people of New York City. Distributing food and finding shelter and employment for the poor became her prime concern. She dedicated herself to the cause so thoroughly that she soon became known as "The Protestant Sister of Charity." When she and friend Isabella Graham organized "The Society for the Relief of Poor Widows with Small Children" in 1797, New York was blessed with the first charitable organization in its history.

Elizabeth's husband, William, then suffered severe financial and physical setbacks. Elizabeth went with her husband and their eldest daughter to Italy in the hope that the vacation would restore his health. Unfortunately, the remedy came too late. William died in Italy later that year. Elizabeth was twenty-nine.

Heartbroken, Elizabeth took solace in the Catholic Church. By the time she returned to America almost a year later, she had decided to join the Roman Catholic Church. Because of this decision, most of her Protestant family and friends turned against her. Without money or friends, she tried to make a living but failed. Finally, the Church offered her the opportunity to open a girls' school in Baltimore.

At last Elizabeth could use her skills and share them with others. In the spring of 1809, she and four colleagues formed the first native American religious community, calling themselves the Sisters of St. Joseph. Elizabeth was elected Mother Superior. The school moved to nearby Emmitsburg, and after 1812 the order was called the Sisters of Charity of St. Joseph.

Although the order later became successful, the first few years were difficult. Elizabeth, now known as Mother Seton, be-

256

gan the difficult task of training teachers to become qualified Catholic educators, in addition to giving shelter and food to poor children of the school and neighborhood and spending many long hours in quiet contemplation and prayer.

A strong believer in social welfare, Mother Seton worked tirelessly for her community, mainly through her school, until her death at the age of 46. Eventually, the order she had worked so hard to establish numbered ten thousand women and included a nationwide system of charitable and educational organizations. The country's first Catholic orphanage, maternity hospital, and parish school are just a few of Elizabeth's accomplishments. In 1856, Seton Hall College was named in her honor.

In part because of her life of good works and high moral standing, and in part because the Pope deemed three of her acts to be religious miracles, Mother Seton was canonized on September 14, 1975, as Saint Elizabeth Ann, the first and only native-born American saint.

SITTING BULL (TATANKA YOTANKA)

NATIVE AMERICAN CHIEF

BORN *near Grand River, South Dakota, probably in 1831*

DIED *Grand River, South Dakota, December 15, 1890*

Sitting Bull is perhaps the most famous Native American who ever lived, known as the man who defeated the legendary George Armstrong Custer at the Battle of Little Big Horn. Despite his fame, however, relatively little is known about his personal history, since he lived in a culture that had no written language.

The Sioux were a hunting tribe, expert riders who pursued buffalo and other game over immense tracts of the American West. A Sioux might have to survive for days without eating, and had to move with complete silence to surprise his prey. From an early age, the braves developed incredible powers of ph, ,ical endurance.

Trained as a warrior, by the time he reached the age of fourteen Sitting Bull was known for his fearlessness. This five-foot-eight, powerfully built young man, with a craggy and stern face, grew to be a great leader, respected for his skills both as a fighter and as a political strategist.

The training of a Sioux warrior included the grueling Sun Dance. Metal or bone hooks were stuck into the chests and backs of warriors underneath the muscles. The hooks were then strung up to poles, lifting the warrior up until his feet barely touched the ground. He then danced in this position for days, worshiping the sun and experiencing visions.

When Sitting Bull underwent the Sun Dance, his visions were ominous. He saw the need for the Indians to come together to hold off the advancing white man. He had seen that even among the Sioux there were many different tribes that rarely cooperated when the white man attacked. If they could join together, they might have a chance to keep their homeland from being taken away.

In 1868, much of the Sioux nation agreed to be confined to a reservation around the Black Hills of South Dakota—but Sitting Bull refused. Many Indians joined him when white prospectors swarmed over sacred Sioux burial grounds after gold was discovered there. Instead of honoring the treaty they had forced upon the Indian, the U.S. government ordered the Sioux into yet a smaller area.

Although definite numbers are impossible to know, by 1876 Sitting Bull had gathered about 11,000 Indians, including 4,000 Sioux, Arapaho, and Cheyenne warriors, near the Rosebud and Little Big Horn rivers in Montana. This was probably the biggest congregation of Indians in North America in history.

Still, the Indians did not want war. They were by now aware

that numbers were on the side of the white man, and might have been willing to return to reservations under the right terms. But instead of negotiating, the government sent soldiers.

General Custer was a flamboyant and reckless cavalry officer. In the past, his troops had brutally wiped out several Indian villages, killing women and children as well as warriors. He advanced now on the vast Indian encampment against the advice of his scouts. When he charged, Sitting Bull's forces swarmed out and surrounded the soldiers. In a short, furious fight, they wiped out the entire cavalry force of over two hundred men.

After Little Big Horn, the Indians divided into smaller tribes again. Sitting Bull led his men across the border into Canada, just ahead of the cavalry. Unable to make a life there, he returned to the United States in 1881 and surrendered. There he was imprisoned for two years at an army fort, then, in the summer of 1885, joined Buffalo Bill's Wild West Show. In the East, people flocked to see this legendary character.

Returning to the Sioux reservation in South Dakota, Sitting Bull was closely watched. When it appeared that an uprising was imminent, the white-backed Indian police were sent to arrest him. He reportedly resisted arrest and was shot down and killed.

STEVEN SPIELBERG

FILM DIRECTOR

BORN *Cincinnati, Ohio, December 18, 1947*

Who can swim in the ocean today without images of the shark from *Jaws* creeping into his mind? Who thinks of aliens from outer space in the same way after seeing *E.T.: the Extraterrestrial?* And the adventure and romance of *Raiders of the Lost Ark* has caused an exciting revival of old-fashioned adventure movies. Some of today's most successful and popular films, including the above, were made by a young director who has taken Hollywood and the world by storm.

Steven Spielberg was born in Cincinnati, Ohio, the eldest of four children. Growing up, Steven had the normal interests of young American boys—scouting and baseball for instance—but from a young age had an extraordinary passion for filmmaking. Using his father's 8mm movie camera and his own scripts, he enthusiastically experimented with camera angles and plot lines.

Never a good student, Steven spent as much time as he could watching and making films instead of studying. By the time he moved with his family to San Francisco in his late teens, his grades were so poor he was unable to enter film school. Instead, while studying English at a state college in Los Angeles, he spent every spare moment at the movies, sneaking onto movie sets in Hollywood, and making his own small, low-budget 8mm films.

One of these films, called *Amblin'*, gave Steven his big break. Shown at the Venice and Atlanta film festivals, it impressed the head of Universal's television division, Sidney Sheinberg, who hired Steven to direct television scripts.

It was behind the television camera, directing episodes of "Marcus Welby, M.D.," "The Name of the Game," and other series during the early 1970s, that Steven honed his directorial skills. One made-for-television movie, *Duel*, was considered a masterpiece of the genre, and led to Steven's first feature movie, *The Sugarland Express*, which starred Goldie Hawn and William Atherton.

From there, the sky—and ocean depths—were the only limits for this energetic director. Based on a book by Peter Benchley, *Jaws* terrified summer audiences with its fearsome depiction of a resort community's siege by a killer shark. Two years later, young and old alike marveled at the technical achievements and emotional impact of *Close Encounters of the Third Kind*, which portrayed aliens from outer space as curious, friendly creatures rather than the acid-spitting evildoers we had seen in other films. *E.T.*, an endearing extraterrestrial, would charm moviegoers around the world.

Steven's ability to tell an emotionally involving story while at the same time awing audiences with special effects has earned him the respect of film critics around the world. His first three films alone brought him twelve Academy Award nominations, six Oscars, and millions of dollars, making him one of the youngest, most successful Hollywood directors in history.

Turning his talents to producing as well as directing, Steven's accomplishments include *Raiders of the Lost Ark* and its sequel *Indiana Jones and the Temple of Doom, Poltergeist,* and *1941,* among others. In 1985 Spielberg surprised audiences and critics with *The Color Purple,* a departure from his usual thrillers. Based on the moving book by Alice Walker, *The Color Purple,* a dramatic depiction of a black family in the rural South, earned him a Best Director nomination.

Today, Steven and actress Amy Irving live in Los Angeles with their son, Max. One of the youngest filmmakers to win the Irving G. Thalberg Memorial Award at the 1987 Academy Awards, Steven Spielberg remains, at the young age of forty-two, one of the brightest talents in Hollywood.

263

BENJAMIN SPOCK

PHYSICIAN

BORN *New Haven, Connecticut, May 2, 1903*

"**N**ever hold a child on your lap. Never rock its carriage. If you must, kiss them once on the forehead when they say good night. Shake hands with them in the morning." So read a widely circulated pamphlet put out by the U.S. Children's Bureau in 1928, summing up child-rearing practices that had been recommended to parents for over fifty years. Benjamin Spock, then a young pediatrician, turned that advice upside down when he published *The Common Sense Book of Baby and Child Care* in 1946 which disputed such teachings.

In this book, he encouraged parents to treat their children like human beings, to hold and kiss them often. He also reassured parents by telling them, "You know more than you think you do," and urged them to use common sense and instinct rather than any elaborate philosophy when raising their children. Within a year of its publication, Dr. Spock's landmark book was transforming the lives of millions of American families, and his influence remains strong today.

Benjamin's own childhood holds a clue to his theories. Descendants of Dutch immigrants, the Spocks lived in an upper middle-class neighborhood in New Haven, Connecticut. Benjamin's parents, Benjamin and Mildred, were quite strict and frequently inflicted harsh physical punishment on them. Benjamin grew up obedient and intimidated by authority.

Benjamin excelled in school, attending the prestigious preparatory school Phillips Exeter Academy in Andover, Massachusetts. His love for athletics led him to join the rowing team when he entered Yale in 1921. He and the team would win the Gold Medal in the 1924 Olympics in Paris. Throughout his life, he would remain an avid rower, figure skater, and bicyclist.

The fact that his mother adored infants inspired Benjamin to specialize in pediatrics at Yale Medical School and Columbia University's College of Physicians and Surgeons after graduating from Yale in 1925. The turning point in his life came when he took off a year to study psychiatry. Although at that time pediatrics and psychiatry were not seen as related fields, Benjamin wanted to understand why his parents had brought him up the way they did and how it had affected him.

When he opened his own practice, he began to see different ways to deal with children. Although his many delighted patients and their parents adored his soft-spoken manner and easy smile, Benjamin once remarked in the *New York Times* that one of his faults "has always been that I whoop it up too much with chil-

265

dren." His office was filled with toys and gadgets for his young patients to play with and his own warmth made them feel comfortable, even in a doctor's office.

Reading the standard child care books of the day, Benjamin was disappointed in both their content, which encouraged strictness rather than flexibility, and their tone, which lectured to parents. When he wrote his own book he tried "to be supportive of parents rather than to scold them. Instead of just telling a parent what to do, I usually tried to explain what children are like at different stages of development . . . so that the parent would know what to expect and could act on his own knowledge." In this way, a new approach to parenting was born.

In addition to his pioneering work in pediatrics, Benjamin is also known for his political activism, particularly his support for the anti-Vietnam War movement in the 1960s. He himself has been arrested in demonstrations over a dozen times. Now a supporter of the antinuclear movement, he is still a popular lecturer on college campuses and in other forums.

Today, at eighty-five, Dr. Spock remains active politically and is a parent of two and grandparent of several children himself.

BRUCE SPRINGSTEEN

ROCK MUSICIAN, COMPOSER

BORN *Freehold, New Jersey, September 23, 1949*

❝**I** saw rock and roll's future and its name is Bruce Springsteen," wrote reporter and record producer Jon Landau in 1975. Soon after, fans and rock critics the world over would share the same kind of enthusiasm about "the Boss." Today, Bruce is still at the top of the charts and is one of the most popular performers and accomplished songwriters in rock and roll history.

Bruce grew up in Freehold, a small town on the New Jersey shore, which was once a fancy resort area but has declined in recent years. Bruce is the oldest child of Adele and Douglas Springsteen and has two sisters, Ginny and Pam.

Entranced by Elvis Presley and other 1950s rock and roll-ers, Bruce scraped together enough money to buy a beat-up used guitar when he was just thirteen. "From the beginning," Bruce recalled in *Time,* "my guitar was something I could go to. If I hadn't found music, I don't know what I would have done." Ex-pressing the loneliness and rebelliousness he felt in his own teen years in his music, Bruce composed some highly emotional lyrics driven by the rock 'n' roll rhythms of his idols.

A year later, he'd taught himself to play the guitar, piano, and harmonica well enough to play in local bands performing in clubs around the Jersey shore. When he finished high school he began his career in earnest, belonging to a number of different bands. He performed as often as he could, and anywhere from trailer parks to shopping center parking lots to local clubs and firemen's balls. All the while, Bruce was developing an original rock-and-roll style. Dancing, jumping, and singing with intense emotion, Bruce set his concert audiences on fire.

At the same time, his songwriting also developed. Themes of youthful alienation and independence, though still significant, be-gan to be overshadowed by more socially conscious messages. Unemployment, hunger, poverty, and the tragedy of war have become important issues in today's world, and Bruce's music has spoken to those issues with compassion and hope. Songs like "My Hometown," which describes a depressed steel mill city, and "Born in the U.S.A.," a song about the plight of Vietnam veter-ans in this country, bring attention to these problems in a unique way.

Bruce's concern for the disadvantaged and alienated reaches far beyond his lyrics. He has donated his time and money, pub-licly and privately, to a number of different efforts to feed the hungry of America and the world. He performed on "We Are the World," a fund-raising record and video to help famine victims in Africa. He has worked toward the cause of nuclear disarmament

268

by participating in charitable concerts and rallies all over the country. And quietly, with little fanfare, Bruce has personally given money to food banks, unemployed steelworkers, the homeless, drug-abuse treatment centers, and other groups and individuals in need.

Though Bruce has become a very wealthy and famous man, he still lives modestly on the Jersey shore. Bruce has recorded nine albums, sales of which total nearly 20 million copies. From his first, "Greetings from Asbury Park, New Jersey," produced in 1973, to his latest, "Tunnel of Love," released in 1987, Bruce Springsteen's music has been received with great enthusiasm by fans and critics alike.

GLORIA STEINEM

JOURNALIST, FEMINIST LEADER

BORN *Toledo, Ohio, March 25, 1936*

To many people, Gloria Steinem is a symbol of today's woman—successful, powerful, and attractive. The magazine she founded in 1972, *Ms.*, is a symbol, too, of the enormous strides women have made in terms of political power and equality over the last fifteen years. It has been a struggle, however, both for Gloria and the women's movement *Ms.* represents.

Gloria Steinem was born in 1936 to Ruth and Leo Steinem and much of her childhood was spent in poverty. Her father was a traveling antiques dealer who took his family with him in a trailer as he tried to sell his wares across the country. Gloria was about twelve years old when her parents divorced and her mother took a job as a newspaper reporter in Toledo, Ohio. Although Ruth Steinem was employed, she was poorly paid, and the family lived in a slum.

Despite the fact that Gloria and her older sister, Susanne, now could attend school regularly for the first time, it was not a happy period. Gloria never did well in school; in fact she left high school in her senior year. But because she scored well on an entrance exam, she was admitted to Smith College in Northampton, Massachusetts.

There her intelligence and gift for writing came alive. She excelled at Smith, winning several scholarships and graduating with an honors degree in government and a decision to make journalism her career.

Gloria moved to New York in 1960 to begin her career as a journalist and free-lance writer. In 1962, when she wrote an article about the changing sexual values in America, entitled "The Moral Disarmament of Betty Coed," for *Esquire* magazine, she drew attention from editors and readers across the country. In this article, Gloria wrote for the first time on themes that later become the focus of her career—the problems of women in the modern world.

That assignment led to others for *Esquire, Vogue, Life,* and other prestigious journals. Although her interests focused on investigative reporting, she was usually assigned "light" material— human interest stories and celebrity interviews, assignments almost always given to women in the male-dominated journalistic world.

At the same time her career was blossoming, Gloria's concerns were focusing more and more on the politics of the day, especially the anti-war and civil rights movements. Although Gloria had written often on women's issues, her involvement in the feminist movement didn't really begin until 1968, when she attended a feminist group's meeting in New York City. She told a reporter in 1971, "Before that meeting, I had thought that my personal problems and experiences were my own and not part of a larger political problem."

Equal pay for equal work, opportunities for growth outside the home, respect and dignity for all women were rallying cries of the feminist movement, and Gloria became a most effective spokeswoman. Her leadership in a number of women's groups, including the National Organization of Women, making demands for laws against discrimination toward women, especially the Equal Rights Amendment, put her at the forefront of political change.

In 1972, Gloria helped found a new women's magazine, one that would, as Gloria later characterized it, serve as a how-to for women—"not how to make jelly but how to seize control of your life." Since that time, *Ms.* has served the needs of many American women who today have more choices than ever before. Articles about finances and educational opportunities, family planning and the challenges for working mothers have made *Ms.* an important resource.

Today, Gloria sees the roles for men and women continuing to evolve. In a recent interview in *Esquire,* she said: "Progress for women lies in becoming more assertive, more able to deal with conflict, and becoming more active outside the home. Progress for men will be in becoming more empathetic, more compassionate, more comfortable working inside the home. . . . We're not just trading places. . . . We can all be allies."

TECUMSEH

INDIAN LEADER

BORN *near Oldtown, Ohio, March ?, 1768*

DIED *Thamesville, Ontario, October 5, 1813*

Not much is known about the childhood of the great Shawnee chief, Tecumseh, but it can be said with certainty that he had
a profound effect on his people and their history.

Both his parents were Shawnee, his father a chief who was
killed at the battle of Point Pleasant in 1774. The Shawnee tribe,
like all other Native Americans, were being pushed off their land
by the white settlers from Europe. Once inhabiting what is now
Ohio, the tribe was forced farther and farther into what is now
Indiana while Tecumseh was growing up. Constant battles raged

Tecumseh at the moment of his death

between the whites and the Indians, and by the time Tecumseh reached adulthood he too was considered a fine warrior, and was made chief of his tribe.

The white man was a clever enemy, and knew how to trick the Indians into relinquishing more and more of their homeland. Approaching the different tribes separately, the settlers could overpower the Indians, either with treaties which were later broken or through battle. Tecumseh realized that the only chance the Indians had to overcome the white man would be to unite. His theory was that the land belonged to all the Indians together, and that no agreement could be made with the white man unless all the tribes agreed. Implicit in this theory was that if the white man went back on his part of the deal, which was not uncommon, all the tribes would fight together as one Indian nation. Together, they would have power they did not have separately. In this way, they could keep the land they had nurtured and lived on for centuries.

Tecumseh and his brother, the religious leader Tenskwatawa, also known as the Prophet, worked together to unite the Indians. The Prophet preached to the Indians of their rich culture and traditional self-sufficiency, which had been overshadowed by an increasing dependence on the white man for their clothing and military weapons. Chiefs were being manipulated by United States agents, who plied them with liquor and other gifts, and the Prophet worked hard to restore the Indians' pride and independence.

At the same time Tecumseh traveled throughout the nation, hoping to attract people to his theory and bring them to live at Tippecanoe, a village he created along the Wabash River near the mouth of Tippecanoe in Indiana. He was a tall, lean man with a light copper complexion and handsome face. He spoke with a power that made a profound impression on all who heard him.

More and more Indians, from many different tribes, joined him in his dream of a united Indian nation.

Unfortunately, however, Tenskwatawa was not nearly as practical as his brother. He relied on mysticism to guide him, and his instincts were not always correct. Tecumseh warned him never to allow the tribe to be drawn into battle while Tecumseh was away, as this would surely lead to disaster. But while Tecumseh was bringing his plan for peace to tribes in the Southeast, Tenskwatawa decided to attack Territorial Governor William Henry Harrison—Tecumseh's greatest enemy—and his troops, who had gathered outside Tecumseh's camp, clearly instigating a battle. The Indian village was devastated, and the warriors who were not killed scattered across the state. Tecumseh's carefully constructed confederacy was virtually destroyed.

Still hoping to save his land and his people from being further ravaged, Tecumseh placed his hope, but never his trust, with the British, who would soon fight the Americans in the War of 1812. Fighting bravely alongside the British, he was cruelly disappointed when he discovered their plan to retreat from the region, leaving the Indians once again alone and unprotected. Despite his misgivings, he joined them as they retreated into Canada, fighting his last battle near the Thames River, where he was killed by an American soldier.

275

HARRY TRUMAN

PRESIDENT

BORN *Lamar, Missouri, May 8, 1884*
DIED *Kansas City, Missouri, December 26, 1972*

"The Buck Stops Here" read the famous sign on President Harry Truman's desk—a fitting slogan for one of the most fiery leaders in American history. A President almost by accident, he was ultimately responsible for decisions that made a huge difference in how our world is shaped today.

As a child, Harry was prone to accident and illness. A case of diphtheria left him briefly paralyzed at the age of nine. He was always very nearsighted and wore thick glasses from the age of seven or eight. Because the glasses were expensive for his family,

President Harry Truman, his wife Bess, and daughter Margaret

Harry was forbidden to play most sports. Forced to stay at home, he became an avid reader and a companion to his younger sister.

Although he was a good student, there was no money for Harry's education after high school, and he instead took over his grandmother's farm. But, returning to Missouri after serving in World War I as a captain of artillery, he moved to Independence and married his longtime sweetheart, Bess Wallace. It was a happy marriage, one that lasted his lifetime and captured the hearts of America.

Harry then turned to politics. He was elected a county judge, then elected to the U.S. Senate, where he served two terms. In 1944, President Franklin D. Roosevelt chose him to run as Vice President.

Despite his failing health, President Roosevelt won a record fourth term, but died only three months into it. Harry took over —an unimposing political unknown—and many people predicted disaster.

Few other new presidents have had to make so many crucial decisions so quickly. Within four months of taking office, he approved the atomic bomb attacks that forced the surrender of Japan. Unlike many people at the time, he recognized the dangers of this powerful new weapon, but used it because he felt an invasion of Japan would have cost many more lives on both sides.

277

This momentous action was only the beginning. At home, millions of returning veterans sought jobs, education, and housing, and black Americans were beginning the long, hard struggle for civil rights. Harry's answer to domestic problems was the "Fair Deal" program, which had as its goals an increase in the minimum wage, the desegregation of the Armed Forces, and the replacement of slums with thousands of new, low-cost houses.

Perhaps President Truman's greatest accomplishments, however, came in foreign policy. Much of Europe was still devastated by World War II. Knowing it would take both military and economic aid for Western Europe to resist the pressure of the Soviet Union, his administration came up with the NATO military alliance and the Marshall Plan. Under the plan, the United States invested $17 billion in Europe's economies. This not only saved democratic government in Europe, but helped lead to decades of prosperity there and in the United States.

Harry's firm stands against the Soviets and for civil rights had badly divided the Democratic Party, which was not ready to consolidate behind these issues. It looked as if he could not win against Republican candidate Thomas Dewey, but when the votes were in, Truman had scored an amazing victory.

His elected term in office was fraught with new challenges. Senator Joseph McCarthy led attempts to smear many members of Truman's administration as Soviet spies or sympathizers. And the United States became embroiled in another war, trying to keep Soviet-backed North Korea from conquering South Korea.

Harry resisted demands that he use nuclear weapons against the North Koreans and got the support of the United Nations behind South Korea, and that country was saved from conquest. And in perhaps the most controversial move of his exciting career, he recalled General Douglas MacArthur, a national hero, for disobeying orders.

After his term ended, later presidents often sought Harry's advice. He became a beloved figure, admired as an ordinary American who became great when he had greatness thrust upon him.

HARRIET TUBMAN

ABOLITIONIST

BORN *Dorchester County, Maryland, c. 1820*

DIED *Auburn, New York, March 10, 1913*

"When I found I had crossed the [Mason-Dixon] line, I looked at my hands to see if I were the same person . . . the sun came like gold through the tree and over the field and I felt like I was in heaven."

Harriet Tubman, born a slave, had finally escaped the chains that bound her. For all her twenty-nine years on earth, she had been treated like a piece of property by white men and women who believed that human beings could be "owned." She had toiled under a hot sun in the fields of Maryland, praying she did not get beaten for not working hard enough.

Harriet never endured the reins of slavery peacefully. Although much information about her early life has been lost or poorly documented, one story recalled often tells of an injury young Harriet received while helping save a fellow slave from a beating. A two-pound iron weight was thrown at her as she blocked the doorway to keep the master from chasing the slave. The metal struck Harriet in the forehead, knocking her unconscious and leaving an indentation in her skull. She never altogether recovered from this wound; she suffered three or four blackouts a day for the rest of her life.

When Harriet heard that she and her family would be sent farther south, where conditions were even worse, she decided to make the treacherous journey north—to freedom. Other runaway slaves who had been captured and sent back south had told her of the Underground Railroad. This was a series of houses, tunnels, and roads set up by abolitionists—white men and women who wished to do away with slavery and bring as many black people as they could into freedom.

After a difficult journey on this highly secret route, Harriet made it all the way to Philadelphia, Pennsylvania, and freedom. Working as a maid, finally being paid for her services, Harriet saved every penny she could, knowing she would need money to help in the fight to free her brothers and sisters. She planned to join the Underground Railroad and help the abolitionists in their work.

Her first expedition took place in 1851, when she managed to thread her way through the South, risking death, to take her sister and her sister's children north from Baltimore. From that time until the onset of the Civil War, Harriet led one expedition after another, her reputation growing with each successful adventure. Black people referred to her as Moses, the prophet who could lead them into the promised land.

Using clever disguises and unmatched courage, Harriet's

methods became more and more refined. In the fifteen years Harriet worked on the Railroad, she personally supervised the escapes of some 300 slaves.

During the Civil War, Harriet worked as a nurse, cook, and sometime spy for the Union Army. She also took part in a military expedition that resulted in the rescue of 756 former slaves and destroyed millions of dollars' worth of enemy property.

Unfortunately the Emancipation Proclamation, which freed the slaves, did not eliminate racism and prejudice against her people. In fact, Harriet herself could not receive proper military benefits because she was black, and she spent the rest of her life in poverty.

But her work never ceased. Some fifteen years before she died, she set up a shelter to house the aged and destitute, scrimping together whatever money she could. Harriet Tubman toiled and suffered so that others could enjoy freedom. She died on March 10, 1913.

ANDY WARHOL

ARTIST, FILMMAKER, PUBLISHER

BORN *Pittsburgh, Pennsylvania (?), August 6, 1928 (?)*
DIED *New York, New York, February 22, 1987*

The name Andy Warhol at once conjures up images of controversy, mystery, violence and creativity. His sudden death in 1987, at the approximate age of 59, inspired even more speculation about his lifestyle, his wealth, his celebrity status, and especially his contributions as an artist. Despite such controversy, he will be forever remembered as the man who ushered in the Pop era of the 1960s—a mixture of art and outrageous behavior.

Even his childhood remains a mystery. No one is quite sure of his birthday; both the year and the day are in doubt. Some biographical material suggests he was born in Pittsburgh or Philadelphia, others in McKeesport, Pennsylvania. It is almost certain, however, that he was one of three sons of Czech immigrants and his name was originally Warhola.

Andy attended the Carnegie Institute of Technology (now Carnegie-Mellon University) and received his degree in pictorial design in 1949. After graduation, he changed his name to Warhol and headed straight for New York City. There he began a lucrative career as a free-lance advertising illustrator for such magazines as *Vogue, Harper's,* and *Glamour.*

Although a very successful commercial artist, Andy was striving for something else in his career. In 1960, he began a new and groundbreaking phase in his artistic development. Along with other modern artists, including Roy Lichtenstein and James Rosenquist, Andy started to experiment with figures from American popular culture—including comic-book characters like Superman and Dick Tracy.

About 1962, Andy developed his own particular trademark when he painted a series of Campbell's soup cans. To Andy, the soup can was as fit a subject for art as any other still-life object. 283 The painting became a great sensation and Andy used this same kind of repetitive motif to portray other common household goods.

Eventually he stopped painting entirely and developed new techniques that used the easily reproducible silk-screen method. Focusing now on portraits made from photographs, Andy's depictions of such celebrities as Marilyn Monroe and Jacqueline Kennedy were extremely popular. Impersonal and consistently precise, they were used by Andy as a symbolic representation of a society he felt lacked humanity and compassion.

As his fame as an artist grew, Andy insisted that money, not art, was all that interested him. "Art is a man's name," he once proclaimed. Calling his studio "The Factory," Warhol reinforced the idea that his works were indeed no more than "products" of an industrial machine.

In the mid-1960s, Andy turned his talents to filmmaking as well. Films like *Eat, Haircut, Sleep,* and *Empire* were made to be purposely boring and static, as a comment on the society watching them.

In the meantime, The Factory had become populated by other would-be artists and filmmakers. Some would go on to careers of their own, while others were there only to use drugs and bask in Andy's fame.

Such an atmosphere was bound to erupt in violence, and in 1968 Andy was shot by an actress who once had worked at The Factory. After recuperating for a year, Andy turned his energies to a new project, *Interview* magazine, a journal that features celebrity interviews and up-to-the-minute fashions.

Through the 1970s and 1980s, Andy continued to produce silk-screen images of popular entertainers and public figures. A versatile figure who confounded critics and fans alike, Andy Warhol was a symbol of both intellectual creativity and surface celebrity. Although his contributions will last for generations, he will always be remembered as the man who said, "In the future, everyone will become world-famous for fifteen minutes."

284

GEORGE WASHINGTON

PRESIDENT, SOLDIER

BORN *Westmoreland County, Virginia, February 22, 1732*

DIED *Mount Vernon, Virginia, December 14, 1799*

"First in war, first in peace, and first in the hearts of his countrymen." For nearly two hundred years, Americans have used these words to describe our first President—a man whose bravery on the Revolutionary battlefield was matched by his skills as a diplomat and politician.

George never chopped down a cherry tree on his father's farm; in fact most of the tales about his childhood are myths. His parents died when he was quite young, and after that he was shuttled back and forth between relatives in northern Virginia.

George Washington (center of photo)

Eventually, George was taken in by his half brother, from whom he inherited the family's farm in Mount Vernon, Virginia.

With only seven or eight years of schooling, it was up to George to supplement his education. He loved to read, and by the time he was fifteen he had taught himself a trade by making maps and traveling through rough, Indian-inhabited woods to become a land surveyor.

Volunteering for a famous mission during the French and Indian War, George began his long career in the military. To warn the French off land that England had claimed, George and his unit were forced to cross hundreds of miles of untamed and hostile territory in the dead of winter. On the journey he was shot at, nearly drowned, and came close to freezing. The trip, however, was to no avail, and George would spend the next four years fighting alongside English soldiers until the French finally gave up.

After the war, George ran his successful farm at Mount Vernon and served in the colonial legislature. He married Martha Custis, a widow, and helped to raise her children. The marriage was apparently a happy one, lasting the rest of his life.

286

An important and wealthy man in Virginia, George was elected to the First Continental Congress, which met to outline a strategy for the colonies to deal with England. Because of his previous military experience, George was selected after the Second Continental Congress to head the new army against the British when more peaceful means of negotiating a settlement failed. The delegates were also impressed by his military bearing. At six-foot-two, Washington towered over most men of his time, and usually appeared very serious, rarely smiling. His solemn expression may have been due to his bad false teeth, which were made out of wood.

George faced a nearly impossible job. England's army was probably the best in the world, manned with professional soldiers who had years of experience. The colonials were untrained and poorly equipped. George himself had never commanded a force of this size, and had to do much of his learning as he went along.

Many of the colonists, at first enthusiastic, despaired as the war dragged on. Often it was only George's own personal determination and resourcefulness—he served without pay throughout the war—that kept the army together through such terrible times as when they endured a harsh winter at Valley Forge without enough food or fuel.

George made mistakes, but often proved to be a daring and skillful commander. When the odds were in his favor he fought hard, and when he was hopelessly outnumbered he retreated to save his men. Finally, with the help of French allies, he defeated the British at the battle of Yorktown and ensured America's freedom.

After the war, George was soon involved in politics again. He was elected to preside over the Constitutional Convention, which devised this nation's unique Constitution, tying the former colonies together at a crucial time. Fittingly, George was then elected the first President of the United States.

287

George was as conscientious a President as he had been a general. He refused to take sides in the quarrels of Britain and France, the world's superpowers at the time, and tried to establish fair and democratic laws for running his new nation.

After two terms, George insisted on returning home. When war with France threatened to erupt a few years later, though, he reluctantly took charge of the army again. Happily, war was averted and "the father of his country" died in peace the following year, at his beloved Mount Vernon at the age of sixty-seven.

NOAH WEBSTER

LEXICOGRAPHER

BORN *West Hartford, Connecticut, October 16, 1758*

DIED *New Haven, Connecticut, May 28, 1843*

The first of its kind created in the United States, *An American Dictionary of the English Language* was published in 1828, after its author spent over twenty years compiling its words, pronunciations, and definitions. Today, over 160 years later, this book, updated on a continuing basis, remains one of the finest English dictionaries ever produced.

It was largely due to the efforts of Noah Webster that America began to explore its own language. It was he who wrote the first comprehensive grammar and vocabulary texts, models for grammar and spelling books we use today.

Born to one of Connecticut's founding families, Noah grew up on a modest farm in what is now West Hartford. Although his father, Noah Sr., was a prestigious member of the parish church, a justice of the peace, and a captain of the local militia, the Websters were not at all a wealthy family.

Throughout his childhood Noah was a bright and eager learner, harboring a special passion for reading and writing. Language fascinated him, and after completing as much schooling as West Hartford could offer him, he begged his father to send him to college—an expensive proposition even in those days. Mortgaging part of the family farm to pay tuition, Noah Sr. managed to enroll his son in Yale College in New Haven.

After graduating from Yale four years later—with time off for a stint in the Revolutionary Army in 1777—Noah decided to become a lawyer. Teaching and clerical work paid his bills while he studied for the bar examination, which he passed in 1781. After four years of active practice, Noah left the law to pursue his true vocation—the study and documentation of the English language.

This career began in 1782 when, while teaching school in 289 Goshen, New York, Noah found the schoolbooks used there to be inadequate. He felt that these textbooks were old-fashioned and didn't take into account the needs of the American student. Originally written and published in England, they did not include many of the new words that had evolved in America. Noah knew that language was always changing according to the needs of the community that spoke it, especially in this new land where so many different cultures and languages mingled. Understanding this principle, Noah undertook the study of American language and education.

By most historical accounts, Noah Webster was not an easy man to like. He was reported to be a vain, intense and argumentative man. But he did much to help our young country politically and scientifically, as well as educationally. An ardent Federalist, he wrote many articles and spoke at rallies in favor of a strong central government. When he wished to protect his work from being copied by others, he helped the new government develop strict copyright laws. He wrote important papers on economics, medicine, and the physical sciences which placed him among the most learned men of his day. He died at the age of eighty-four in New Haven.

Like so many others of his generation, Noah Webster was a man endowed with a great deal of energy. America was a brand-new nation and there was much to do to make it grow. Although we know him best for the dictionary that still bears his name, his accomplishments in other fields and his influence on the political scene should not be underestimated. Without Noah Webster, our language and our country might be quite different today.

WALT WHITMAN

POET

BORN *West Hills, New York, May 31, 1819*
DIED *Camden, New Jersey, March 26, 1892*

More than any other writer, Walt Whitman captured the spirit of a young America, his poetry celebrating the ideals of democracy and equality to which this new nation aspired. Through Walt Whitman's loving eyes, the beauty of nature and man's place within it was expressed in a whole new way.

Walt was born in West Hills, Long Island, but grew up in Brooklyn, New York, after his family moved there when he was three. Walt felt at home both in Brooklyn's crowded streets and at the Long Island shore, to which he made frequent trips. He wrote in his autobiography, "I loved, after bathing, to race up and down the hard sand, and declaim Homer or Shakespeare to the surf and sea gulls by the hour."

Walt left school at about twelve, and became an office boy for the Long Island *Patriot*. It was through this job that he first became involved in the newspaper business. Like other great American writers—Benjamin Franklin, Mark Twain, and Ernest Hemingway, to name a few—he would make journalism his second career. He would spend many years behind the editor's desk of a number of important newspapers.

By the time he was twenty-three, Walt had published a novel, *Franklin Evans*, and had written numerous newspaper articles and editorials. He was an ardent liberal, and became involved in many issues of the day, including temperance and abolition. While helping his work to flourish, Walt's strong political beliefs unfortunately often cost him jobs. When he attacked the Democratic Party for not taking a strong stand against slavery, for instance, he was fired from the editorship of the Brooklyn *Eagle*.

In 1855 Walt published, at his own expense, the first edition of *Leaves of Grass*, a volume of poems that astonished the literary world with its freewheeling themes of man's freedom in nature and equality among men. In twelve poems including the now famous "Song of Myself," Walt wrote about the joy of being human, celebrating all of man's experiences—laughter and tears, birth and death, joy and sadness, love and hate.

For these remarkable poems, Walt experimented with radically new verse forms. He broke away from stylized, metered verse and, in keeping with his own vision of freedom, his poetry lost all trace of convention. Believing that poetry should be a spontaneous experience for both the writer and the reader, he used slang words, coinages, and foreign phrases, attempting to capture the rhythms of everyday language and life.

Leaves of Grass and the many other poems that followed were not particularly well received by either the public or the literary critics of the day. Many found Walt Whitman's writing to be vulgar and obscene and frequently denounced his work. But his reputation as a writer and a controversial figure continued to grow.

When the Civil War broke out and his brother George was wounded at the front, Walt immediately left Brooklyn and volunteered as a nurse in Washington, D.C. He spent eleven years there, writing and working in various jobs after the war.

In January 1873, Walt suffered a stroke that temporarily paralyzed him, prompting him to leave Washington to live with his brother in Camden, New Jersey. A short time later, his mother died. His illness and grief were blows from which he never recovered. For his remaining nineteen years he lived quietly, writing and occasionally lecturing on his poetry and social philosophy. He died on March 26, 1892, leaving the world a truly original legacy.

E L I
W H I T N E Y

I N V E N T O R ,   M A N U F A C T U R E R

B O R N *Westboro, Massachusetts, December 8, 1765*

D I E D *New Haven, Connecticut, January 8, 1825*

Although almost everyone can identify Eli Whitney as the creator of the cotton gin, few realize today the astounding impact that invention had on the agricultural life of the nineteenth century.

Raised on a farm in Connecticut, Eli was educated in local primary schools. When his father opened a manufacturing shop on the farm shortly before the Revolutionary War, Eli pitched in to help in his spare time. During the war, the Whitneys wisely installed a metal furnace to produce nails and other high-priced metalworks. After the war, they turned to manufacturing a variety of metal objects used in daily peacetime life, including hat pins and clips.

While Eli was talented at running the machinery in his father's shop, his ambitions went far beyond the Whitneys' charming farm in Massachusetts. Determined to attend college, he both worked to earn tuition and studied hard until he was finally accepted into Yale College. By the time he graduated, at age twenty-seven, he had learned not only the specifics of mechanics in general, but also the new technologies then being developed in Europe.

After graduation, Eli attempted to teach in New Haven, but was unable to find work. He was offered a position as a private tutor in South Carolina. On his way to his new job, Eli visited a friend, Phineas Miller, who managed the Mulberry Grove plantation in Georgia.

There Eli became fascinated with cotton picking and processing. At the time, it took one whole day to clean the sharp, sticky seeds from the fibers of just one pound of cotton. Eli realized that a faster, more economical way to clean cotton was needed. Recalling his training in mechanics, he quickly came up with a simple device that would speed up the process considerably. With support from Miller, Eli won a patent on his cotton gin in 1794.

Although Eli's intentions were honorable, his invention was ultimately used to promote the slave trade, upon which the Southern cotton industry was based. The cotton gin was partially responsible for an additional sixty years of slavery in the United States.

Despite receiving a patent for the cotton gin Eli never benefited financially from his invention, as numerous other entrepreneurs copied his machines. What little money he did make he used to foster other inventions, which finally led to both financial reward and personal satisfaction.

In 1798 he and Miller collaborated on a gun manufacturing process, by which guns could be mass-produced instead of hand-crafted. Moving back to his home state of Connecticut, Eli opened his own factory. Until that time it was impossible for any manufacturer to turn out more than 250 guns a year. But Eli's process allowed his company to fill 10,000 musket orders from the United States Government in eight years.

When Eli died at the age of fifty-nine, he left behind an America well into its Industrial Revolution, the legacy of which are the factories and mass-produced goods we take for granted today.

FRANK LLOYD WRIGHT

ARCHITECT

BORN *Richland Center, Wisconsin, June 8, 1869*
DIED *Phoenix, Arizona, April 9, 1959*

Perhaps no man has had more of an influence on twentieth-century architecture than Frank Lloyd Wright. Designing homes, offices, museums, hotels, churches, and even casinos, he conquered nearly all of the great problems facing modern builders with a unique style.

Frank grew up in Massachusetts and Wisconsin. His childhood years included some time spent on his uncle's farm, where he first enjoyed "the freshness of the earth itself" that was to influence his architecture. With a friend, he ran a basement printing operation. By laying out publications, he learned the basic elements of design.

Frank's mother always encouraged him to become an architect. Since the University of Wisconsin did not offer any courses in the subject, he majored in engineering there before leaving, without graduating, to work at an architectural firm in Chicago for eight dollars a week. He was subsequently given a five-year contract at another firm that made it possible for him to marry his first wife, Catherine Tobin, and begin his work as a designer in earnest.

By 1900 Frank was working on his first revolutionary designs, his "Prairie Houses." These houses include features that would become Wright trademarks, including mass-produced materials used to achieve comfortable, convenient houses for reasonable prices. Rooms were large and flowed smoothly into each other. The interior was designed to relate in style to the outside landscape, and each house fit into its unique natural environment.

Frank then brought his creative vision to office buildings. He designed the first building in the United States to use metal-bound plate-glass doors and windows. He was the first architect to use poured concrete in large public buildings, and early in the 1920s, he pioneered the use of precast concrete blocks with reinforcing metal rods—all of which were necessary to sustain modern skyscrapers.

His work would be much admired in Europe, where he lived, worked, and lectured for several years, and soon Frank would attain an international reputation. Unfortunately, his professional success could not overshadow his personal misfortunes. In 1909 he had left his wife for another woman, named Mamah Cheney. When Catherine, with whom he had had six children, refused to give him a divorce, he scandalized the country by living with Mamah anyway.

In 1914 an insane servant murdered Mamah and six others

and set Frank's beautiful Wisconsin home, Taliesin, on fire. Stunned, Frank rebuilt his home, only to see it burned again, a decade later, by lightning. He rebuilt it again, but by this time his popularity had faded and he almost lost Taliesin to his creditors. Most building had ceased during the Great Depression, and Frank eked out a living by lecturing at universities and training apprentices at Taliesin.

When money was available to build again, Frank's career was resurrected. As an answer to urban overcrowding, he invented the concept of "Broadacre City," a design for a decentralized, self-contained community. His answer to the demand for affordable housing was his design for "Usonian" homes—handsome one-story buildings with flat roofs and heated concrete foundations.

The Kaufmann House, a private home built on several levels over a small waterfall, signaled Frank's return as the country's leading architect. Right up to the end of his life, he worked steadily at some of his most massive projects. He completed the plans for what may be his most famous work at the age of eighty-three—the Solomon R. Guggenheim Museum in New York. 299

Frank Lloyd Wright was fond of saying, "Give me the luxuries of life, and I will willingly do without the necessities." But few have been more successful at combining luxury with utility as this prolific American architect.

A N D R E W W Y E T H

P A I N T E R

B O R N *Chadds Ford, Pennsylvania, July 12, 1917*

A unique figure in contemporary American art, Andrew Wyeth has created some of America's best-loved paintings while often ignoring the taste of the art establishment. While many artists and art critics have been focusing on work involving abstract forms, lines, and colors, Andrew Wyeth has been drawing and painting natural, realistic scenes, frequently of rural America.

Andrew is the central figure of one of the most famous artistic families in America. His father, Newell Convers Wyeth, was a well-known illustrator of children's books. *Treasure Island* and

Andrew Wyeth and his sister, mother, and wife (from left to right)

Robin Hood are just two of the books that feature N.C.'s exquisitely detailed drawings.

N.C. moved from New England to the idyllic Pennsylvania farming village of Chadds Ford to study illustration with Howard Pyle, another famous illustrator of the day. It was in Chadds Ford that N.C. and his wife, Carolyn, made their home and brought up their five children.

Andrew, the youngest, his brother, and three sisters were raised in an atmosphere of creativity. His brother, Nathaniel, tinkered endlessly with mechanical things; he later became an inventor and an engineer. One sister, Ann, learned piano at a very young age and today is an admired composer. The other sisters, Henriette and Carolyn, are painters.

Andrew had sinus trouble in childhood, which kept him from attending school. He was tutored privately, which left him much time to wander the hills and valleys of Chadds Ford. In an introduction to a catalogue of his works for the Metropolitan Museum of Art he recalled, "I played alone, and wandered a great deal over the hills, painting watercolors that literally exploded, slapdash over my pages, and drew in pencil or pen and ink in a wild and undisciplined manner."

Because two of his older sisters also showed artistic promise, it wasn't until Andrew was nearly fifteen that his father began to see in his youngest son an exceptional talent. N.C. then brought Andrew under his direct tutelage, teaching him how to use paints properly and helping him to see the special qualities of an object so that he might capture them in a drawing.

After years of study, in 1936 Andrew had his first one-man show, in Philadelphia, and a year later a one-man show at the William Macbeth Gallery in New York City, when he was just twenty years old. Many of the paintings in his New York exhibit were seascapes and watercolor landscapes of the coast of Maine, where the Wyeth family frequently spent the summer months. It was in Maine, at the age of twenty-two, that Andrew met and married Betsy Merle James. They too would live, work, and raise their family in the lush farmland of Chadds Ford.

In 1945 a tragic accident caused a turning point in Andrew's life and work. His father was killed when his car was hit by a train at a railroad crossing in Chadds Ford. The tragedy stirred in Andrew a desire to paint more seriously—to break away from his earlier, undisciplined style. His work began to take on a new quality of emotion that set it apart from other landscape paintings.

Andrew Wyeth was the first artist ever to receive the Presidential Medal of Freedom, given to him by President John F. Kennedy in 1963. Today, Andrew's paintings sell for record sums of money and yet, despite this fame and fortune, he and his family live a simple and comfortable life in Chadds Ford.

CHARLES "CHUCK" YEAGER

AVIATOR

BORN *Myra, West Virginia, February 13, 1923*

"I was so high and so remote, and the airplane was so very quiet that I might almost have been motionless." So Chuck Yeager described one of the most famous flights in history—the one that broke the sound barrier and brought him fame.

Surely one of the most colorful characters in the annals of aviation history, Chuck had skill and courage that extended far beyond this one historic flight. He was also a World War II hero and distinguished Air Force commander.

Chuck grew up in a close family of five, in one of the poorest sections of West Virginia. His father worked drilling natural gas wells, and Chuck inherited much of his own mechanical ability from him.

After graduating from high school, Chuck considered working with his father in the gas fields, but decided instead to join the Army Air Force. The United States was on the brink of World War II, and soon Chuck was at an air base in Nevada preparing for combat.

After training, Chuck was assigned to fight in Europe. After only eight missions, his plane was shot down over France. With help from the French underground, he made a harrowing trip to Spain, during which he narrowly avoided being shot by a German patrol.

After the war, Chuck returned to the United States and married Glennis Dickhouse, whom he had met while in training. They are still married and have four children. Chuck has named each of his many planes "Glamorous Glenn."

Chuck began testing new planes for the Air Force after the war. This was a very dangerous job, but vital for U.S. military defense. The new jet planes, designed to reach phenomenal new speeds, were full of unknown dangers and many test pilots were killed. Chuck himself narrowly escaped death on several occasions. Once, in 1953, the engines on his plane failed and Chuck plunged 51,000 feet—nearly ten miles in just fifty-one seconds—before he could get it to work again.

By 1947, a rocket airplane had been developed that scientists thought could fly faster than the speed of sound—one mile in about five seconds—something that had never been done before. In the past, planes trying to fly that fast had often broken apart, their instruments freezing up. Some pilots were asking thousands of dollars to take such a risk. Chuck Yeager volunteered to fly the new XS-1 plane for his regular Air Force pay.

On October 14, 1947, a B-29 plane flew the XS-1 up to

304

42,000 feet, then let it go. Chuck took off, breaking the sound barrier by traveling 670 miles per hour. He became a celebrity when the Air Force announced the news the following year, but the publicity did nothing to slow Chuck down. He went on risking his life in planes that flew faster and faster. In 1953, he set another speed record of 1,650 miles an hour.

After he left the test flight program, Chuck trained and commanded U.S. pilots all over the world. He retired in 1975 having twice won the Distinguished Flying Cross, the Silver Star, the Purple Heart and other awards for his many years of service, including a Congressional Medal of Honor in 1976. He also received several honorary degrees from West Virginia universities, and on one occasion left the award ceremony in a jet plane, boldly flying it under a low bridge.

In the 1980s, Chuck became famous all over again when Tom Wolfe published *The Right Stuff,* with its thrilling descriptions of Chuck's life as a test pilot. The book was later made into a movie, with Sam Shepard playing Chuck. But through it all, Chuck seems to have remained just another "good old boy" from West Virginia, unchanged by his fame and modest about his accomplishments. 305

INDEX

Boldface page numbers indicate primary discussion of a person

INDEX

INDEX

INDEX

INDEX